RURAL ENGLAND

A NATION COMMITTED TO A LIVING COUNTRYSIDE

Presented to Parliament
by the Secretary of State for the Environment and the Minister of Agriculture,
Fisheries and Food by Command of Her Majesty October 1995

Cm 3016   LONDON:HMSO   £18.90 net

FOREWORD BY THE PRIME MINISTER

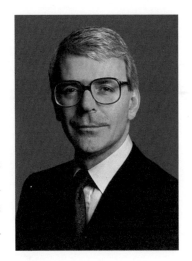

R ural England is the product of human activity over thousands of years, fashioned by the enterprise and endeavour of many generations. It has always been a living countryside. I am determined that it should remain so. Our policies seek to widen opportunity for all and to build prosperity. Yet this must not be at the expense of the wildlife and landscapes we all cherish, and which are our inheritance to pass on to the next generation.

Rural England is not a static place. It has always had to change and adapt to new demands, but the changes of the post-war years have been perhaps the most far reaching in our history. I therefore wanted this White Paper to look at the future of our countryside in its entirety, to examine the changes which have taken place and look for ways to ensure that our rural areas can continue to respond positively to the opportunities which lie ahead as we approach the Millennium. I wanted to explore the practical implications of sustainable development - for rural jobs, for local services, for the environment and not least for people who live in rural areas.

This is the first time ever that Government has undertaken such a comprehensive review. It has involved the whole of Government as well as people across the length and breadth of the country. We all share responsibility for the prosperity of our countryside.

This White Paper will not be the last word. I intend it to mark the beginning of a healthy and open debate about rural England and its future.

John Major

John Major

CONTENTS

INTRODUCTION

The enduring character of England is most clearly to be found in the countryside. Yet the pace of change has quickened and much of what we most value about the rural scene seems threatened by increasing mobility, the pressures of leisure and recreation, the decline of jobs in rural industries and the demands for new jobs in businesses which once would have been found only in the towns.

So this White Paper is about a living and working countryside. It recognises the stresses and strains of widespread change but it never forgets those distinctive qualities whose preservation is a continuing commitment in a country which values the rural way of life.

Of course governments need to approach such an enterprise with humility. The future health of rural England does not rest primarily in their hands, for the countryside is the product of a myriad of human actions over many centuries, moulding the natural world until it is difficult to distinguish what man has created from what nature provided.

Much of what we most value in the natural scene is the product of farming - hillsides whose beauty is dependent upon grazing, water meadows which need to be used for cattle if they are to be preserved, dry stone walls, hedges and traditional buildings. Country sports also have a rôle in conserving the landscape by helping to keep alive copses and woodland. So the White Paper needs to understand this complex interaction between man and nature and look at rural life through the eyes of those who live in the country and not from the administrative perspective of Whitehall.

It began with a wide and open consultation with all the many differing groups who make up our rural communities. That consultation revealed just how extensive was that variety and how different were the priorities and the concerns. No single shift of policy, no universal scheme could provide for all this variety. The reality of life in the countryside is that many small scale changes which respect the real differences in local circumstances are what are most likely to succeed.

For we constantly have to find the balance between competing interests and conflicting concerns. Farmers and foresters who look after 80% of the land; the enthusiasts for our flora and fauna, for ancient buildings and traditional crafts; those who are building the new businesses to replace the old; the incomers who seek to realise their rural idyll; the ramblers and lovers of country sports; those who delight in birds, train horses, or ride the bridleways; landowners and people whose roots run deep in rural England - these and many more have interests which need to be accommodated in a living and working countryside.

County, district and parish councils too, have an important say, while national government, both directly and through the bodies we appoint, needs to develop and protect rural interests. That contribution is important but can only go so far. Working in isolation, none of us can enable the countryside to cope with change. Yet between us we have the talents and resources to ensure both continued rural prosperity and the protection of the character of the countryside. This White Paper sets the scene for a wider debate about how best to achieve this objective.

Consultation

In November 1994 we launched a public consultation to seek people's views on what they thought the White Paper should contain. This exercise was publicised in the national and regional press, and some 380 organisations and individuals responded, most raising more than one issue in their response and some writing to us on more than one occasion. There was a widespread recognition that we should design policies to meet our varied objectives for the countryside in an integrated way, and that local responses to rural needs are often the most appropriate. The main issues raised were:

Economic Development: respondents acknowledged the success of the rural economy over recent years and the importance of continuing economic diversification. Some looked ahead to the new opportunities which modern telecommunications can offer to rural areas.

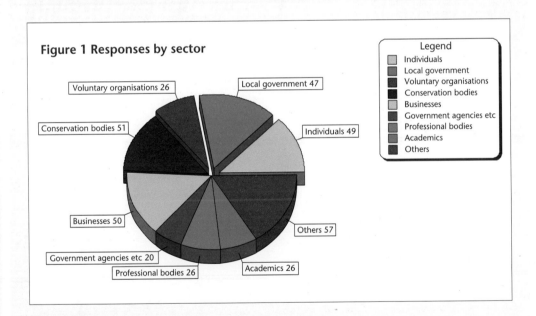

Figure 1 Responses by sector

Legend
Individuals
Local government
Voluntary organisations
Conservation bodies
Businesses
Government agencies etc
Professional bodies
Academics
Others

Voluntary organisations 26
Local government 47
Conservation bodies 51
Individuals 49
Businesses 50
Others 57
Government agencies etc 20
Professional bodies 26
Academics 26

Planning: there was a widespread acknowledgement of the central rôle of planning in enabling development to take place in ways which ensure the continuing economic vitality of the countryside while preserving the quality of its environment. Many emphasised that new developments should be sensitively located and designed.

Rural Services: access to public transport, shops and schools was central to many people's concerns. A significant number of respondents expressed concern about the need for affordable housing in the countryside for local people.

Local Government: many emphasised the potential of parish councils to do more to meet the needs of rural communities, and the scope for greater local involvement in decision making.

Conservation: a majority of respondents wanted to see a greater emphasis on conservation across the countryside and an extension of environmental land management schemes beyond designated areas.

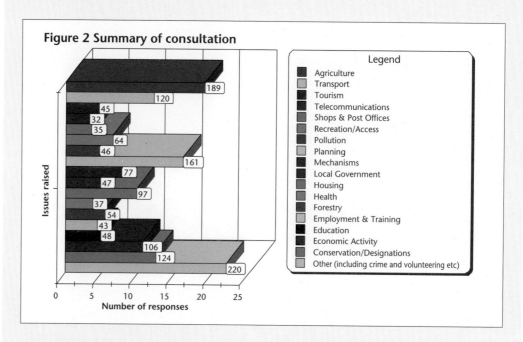

Figure 2 Summary of consultation

Agriculture: whilst many acknowledged the importance of maintaining an efficient agricultural sector, there was a strong consensus that agriculture and the Common Agricultural Policy should deliver more environmental benefits.

In addition to this written consultation, a number of seminars were also held. Some of these, arranged in partnership with local government and the voluntary sector, discussed sectoral issues such as transport, healthcare and forestry and involved experts in the fields under discussion. Others, chaired by Ministers in different regions across the country, discussed a range of issues with a broad cross-section of rural representatives.

BBC Countryfile also ran a series of programmes to coincide with the White Paper consultation, entitled the 'Great Debate'. This generated some 1300 responses from town and country people alike which reinforced the conclusions of the Government's consultation.

National Context

The United Kingdom is one of the most urbanised countries in Europe (see table) and England is the most urbanised part of the Kingdom. Rural England is vulnerable not least because it is so accessible. There is hardly a place in this country which would not fall within the city limits if it were in the United States, hardly a farm more than 30 miles from a major town or city. Rural policy cannot therefore be isolated from other policies.

Figure 3 Comparison of Urban and Rural Areas in Six European Countries

Figures show the percentage of national population living in each of the three types of area.

	Predominantly Rural	Significantly Rural	Predominantly Urban
Netherlands	0	15	85
United Kingdom	15	17	68
Germany	8	26	66
Spain	19	46	35
France	30	41	29
Denmark	39	38	23

This table is based on an OECD standard definition of rurality as an area with a population density of below 150 inhabitants per square kilometre. In each member state specific regions are assessed for degrees of rurality and then split into three categories: predominantly rural, where over 50% of the population lives in rural areas; significantly rural, where 15-50% of the population lives in rural areas; and predominantly urban areas, where under 15% of the population lives in rural areas. In the United Kingdom the regions assessed are based on counties.

People commute from the countryside to cities, and many rural communities depend on visitors from towns. People who work in the countryside now face many of the same challenges as people in towns. A thriving national economy, low inflation, steady growth and free trade are all just as important in villages as in the city centre.

However, there are also important differences between the countryside and towns and cities. We value the English countryside for its distinctive environment and for rural communities which are smaller and more closely knit. These qualities must not be submerged in our predominantly urban culture, nor must the voice of the countryside be drowned by the clamour of our towns and cities.

PRINCIPLES FOR THE COUNTRYSIDE

The Starting Point

The countryside is a **national** asset. The three-quarters of us who live in urban areas value it and enjoy it as visitors and weekenders. Those of us who do not live in the countryside must respect the way of life of those who do, the men and women who live and work there. We must understand and respect their different values and priorities.

Sustainable Development

Sustainable development means managing the countryside in ways that meet current needs without compromising the ability of future generations to meet theirs. This includes:

Zennor, Cornwall

Mike Williams/Countryside Commission

- meeting the economic and social needs of people who live and work in rural areas, ensuring that rural businesses are as efficient and competitive as they can be;

- conserving the character of the countryside - its landscape, wildlife, agricultural, recreational and natural resource value - for the benefit of present and future generations;

- accommodating necessary change while maintaining and enhancing the quality of the environment for local people and visitors;

- encouraging active communities which take the initiative to solve their problems themselves;

- improving the viability of existing villages and market towns by promoting opportunities for both housing and employment, thereby discouraging increased commuting by car to urban centres;

- recognising the interdependence of urban and rural policies, as it is only by encouraging urban regeneration and promoting attractive urban areas that we will reduce unacceptable pressures on the countryside.

Hebden Bridge, Calderdale, West Yorkshire

John Morrison/Environment Picture Library

Dialogue

Often sustainable development manages to please almost everyone. For example, development which is located and designed with sensitivity contributes to local character rather than detracting from it, and the maintenance of beautiful landscapes and abundant wildlife encourages tourism, which generates jobs.

Yet where the pressures of development on the environment are acute, it may be difficult to reconcile competing priorities. Successful resolution of such conflicts requires a willingness on all our parts to appreciate others' perspectives. It requires open dialogue between local communities, local authorities and Government Departments. For its part, the Government must listen to what people in the countryside have to say and respond to their concerns fairly and openly.

Distinctiveness

Responses to the White Paper consultation showed how much we all value the features which make places distinctive. From the sheep rearing uplands of the north Pennines to small coastal communities, from historic market towns to areas of exceptional natural beauty, our approach to rural policies must be flexible and responsive to the defining features of the character of the countryside.

Economic Diversity

From the summit of Pillar Rock towards Great Gable, Lake District

Leeney/Ecoscene

The regional seminars which we held as part of the preparation for this White Paper also showed that each region of the country has its share of more and less remote areas, each with its attendant opportunities and problems. Differences within regions are often greater than differences between them. For example, in rural areas the economy as a whole has performed well. Yet that general fact conceals many particular differences. Those parts of the countryside which are close to large towns have generally done better than more remote areas. On the other hand, they have also experienced more sharply the pressures of growth, higher house prices, intrusive road traffic, demands for retail development, road building and business parks.

Remoter areas often face different challenges. Small communities do not enjoy the choice of shopping or transport which those of us who live in cities take for granted, while lack of access to good roads or railways may make it more difficult for manufacturers to prosper. Sudden changes, such as the closure of a coal mine or defence base, may leave no alternative employment while people have to travel further for training or jobs.

Our policies must therefore recognise the economic and social diversity of the countryside and target programmes on areas of greatest need.

Sound Information

The character of our countryside is not constant. In the last fifty years there have been rapid changes in population, jobs, and the environment, and there is every sign that this will continue well into the next century. If we understand those changes properly we can increase prosperity in the countryside, improve the environment and enhance the quality of life for those of us who live there. Therefore if our policies are to evolve effectively we shall need to improve our understanding of economic, social and environmental trends. Sound science and good information are the only sensible basis for effective action.

OBJECTIVES FOR THE COUNTRYSIDE

Changing Patterns of Work

Rural enterprise creates the prosperity which enables people to enjoy a decent standard of living. It creates the jobs which give young people a future in their communities and the wealth which sustains England's villages and market towns. Our living standards and quality of life depend ultimately on the ability of firms everywhere to create jobs, improve productivity and to win business at home and abroad. Success is earned through increased competitiveness.

Pennine Dales

Today, there is a much greater variety of rural businesses than a few decades ago. As agriculture has become more mechanised, so fewer people work in traditional rural jobs and new jobs in tourism, manufacturing and services have developed. Business location is increasingly a matter of choice rather than necessity and this has given a new diversity which has strengthened the economic base of rural areas and made rural jobs less vulnerable to structural economic change.

Ministry of Agriculture, Fisheries and Food

Figure 4 Changes in Numbers of Employees in Rural and Urban Areas 1981-91[1]

		1981	1991	Change 1981-1991
England	Total	18,382	18,601	219
	Percentage			+1.2%
Rural	Total	3,731	4,217	487
	Percentage	20.3%	22.7%	+13%
Remainder	Total	14,652	14,384	-268
	Percentage	79.7%	77.3%	-1.8%

Source: Census of Employment
Rural is defined as the 150 most rural local authority districts.
Total figures are in 000's

Business development is not incompatible with environmental protection but can be as readily accommodated in rural communities as it was in the heyday of the rural craftsman. New technology has made this possible and enables rural enterprise to benefit from the quality of the countryside environment. Indeed many businesses cite environmental quality as an important reason for locating in rural areas. Furthermore, tourism is now the biggest rural wealth creator and employer. The beauty of the countryside has itself become a key economic resource.

Gary-John Norman/Rural Development Commission

Brimbelow Engineering moved into their new premises at the Old Mill, Catfield, Norfolk in 1993, following restoration part funded by a Redundant Building Grant from the Rural Development Commission

Yet if we want rural enterprises to grow and prosper and make an increasing contribution to national competitiveness, we need to remove barriers to their success and ensure that we provide proper advice, information and training. Our rural economic objectives are:

- to build on the economic success of the countryside;

- to support initiative and avoid placing unnecessary burdens on rural enterprise;

- to encourage further economic diversity by helping to stimulate new and varied forms of wealth creation and employment, especially in areas which have hitherto participated less fully in economic success;

- to promote the exploitation of new technologies which can provide new opportunities for rural people;

- to ensure that development respects the environment in its location, scale and design.

Chapter Two sets out in more detail our policies to encourage the economic competitiveness of the countryside.

[1] *These figures exclude the self employed, those attending work related Government training and members of Her Majesty's Armed Forces.*

Changing Communities

In large towns we generally take easy access to public transport, to nearby shops or to a local doctor's surgery very much for granted. However, this is far from being the case in many rural communities, especially smaller ones, and many parishes have no daily bus service, nor a permanent shop or post office.

Lantern Youth and Community Centre in a converted United Reformed Church, Ilfracombe, Devon

This reflects changes in the way people live and the increased mobility and choice which a majority enjoy through the private car. However the erosion of local services is a problem for those who do not have access to a car, in particular the poor, the young and the elderly.

People should not be left isolated simply because they live in a rural community. Yet no one wants or would be able to replicate urban services in every part of the countryside. Instead if we are to ensure that even in remoter areas people have access to a reasonable and affordable level of essential services, then innovative solutions are demanded.

There is plenty of scope for more shared use of facilities, transport and buildings. Often this can only be achieved with the help of rural people themselves, and this active citizenship cannot be taken for granted - it needs to be worked at and encouraged.

Nor will it be possible unless we use the advent of newcomers to the countryside as an advantage and a resource rather than a problem and a burden. We need to harness their energies and their experience, integrate them more effectively into their chosen communities and ensure that they complement rather than conflict with those who have lived longer in the countryside. By helping to provide affordable housing and stimulating job and leisure opportunities for the young, we can ensure a proper balance in our villages and small towns.

Figure 5 Population Changes in Rural and Urban Areas 1971-91

		1971	1981	1991	Change 1971-1991
England	Total	46,412	46,821	48,208	+1,796
	Percentage				+3.9%
Rural	Total	11,071	12,059	12,936	+1,865
	Percentage	23.9%	25.8%	26.8%	+16.9%
Remainder	Total	35,341	34,761	35,272	-69
	Percentage	76.1%	74.2%	73.2%	-0.2%

Source: Office of Population Censuses and Surveys Mid-Year Population Estimates
Rural is defined as the 150 most rural local authority districts.
Total figures are in 000's

Our objectives for community development are:

- to encourage active communities which are keen to take the initiative to improve their quality of life;

- to reverse the decline in rural services by fostering innovative and flexible ways of meeting local needs;

- to promote living communities, which have a reasonable mix of age, income and occupation, and which offer jobs, affordable housing and other opportunities.

Chapter Three sets out in more detail our policies for delivering services in rural areas.

Changing Environment

The countryside is a priceless part of our national heritage. In the main it has been preserved by generations of landowners and farmers who have been concerned to hand on to the next generation something better than they have themselves taken on. In addition, thanks to our growing appreciation of the value of the countryside, bodies such as the National Trust and the Royal Society for the Protection of Birds have helped to conserve many areas which could otherwise have been lost. Over the past 50 years our efforts have concentrated on those areas which are of outstanding beauty or importance for wildlife. This remains a vital task, but our concern should not be restricted to these areas. Instead, it should also extend to the wider countryside.

Chris King/National Trust Photographic Library

Children from St Martin's School, Scarborough, tending a hedge with wardens at Ravenscar on the Yorkshire coast. The work was undertaken as part of the National Trust's Guardianship Scheme which links schools with particular properties so that pupils can improve their environmental education through site visits and practical work

Whether we live in the town or the country most of us value access to open countryside and woodland. Enjoyment does however take different forms for different people. Some want tranquillity simply to enjoy their surroundings while others prefer to engage in more active and sometimes noisy pursuits. We have to search for ways of reconciling these differing demands.

Technological and economic changes have increased our power to destroy as well as to create. The population of many common birds, for example the song thrush and the skylark, have declined sharply in recent decades. We all share a responsibility to understand why that decline is happening and to reverse it.

The rapid pace of development is putting pressure on some parts of the countryside, especially those close to major towns and cities. Existing urban areas cannot fully accommodate the growing demand for new housing, although re-use of urban land is a key part of our policy. Householders, landowners, local and national government need to work together to identify the most acceptable ways forward, and development needs to contribute to environmental quality in the countryside, not detract from it.

In partnership with farmers, voluntary organisations, developers and local government we would like to see that:

- the distinctive character of rural landscapes and buildings is maintained;

- environmental quality across the countryside is enhanced;

- derelict land is upgraded and restored;

- opportunities for access to the countryside for rural and urban residents alike are improved;

- the decline in the countryside's species of plants and animals is reversed;

- modern pressures for homes, jobs, raw materials, transport and recreation are managed in ways which respect the environment and command public support.

Chapter Four sets out in more detail the Government's policies to conserve and enhance the rural environment for the benefit of local people and as a national resource.

Song Thrush

Skylark at ground nest with young

Roger Wilmshurst/Royal Society for the Protection of Birds

Philip J Newman/Royal Society for the Protection of Birds

THE NATIONAL LOTTERY

Heron Theatre Appeal

The Heron Theatre Appeal was allocated £30,000 from National Lottery funds towards this £70,000 extension to the theatre in Cumbria

National Lottery

Launched in November 1994, the National Lottery has created an important new source of funding for the arts, sport, our national heritage, charities and projects to mark the beginning of the new millennium. Through the five distributing bodies in England, it helps to fund projects which are for the public good and which benefit the community. Both rural and urban areas will benefit.

One of the major themes emerging in projects supported by the Millennium Commission is the enhancement of the natural environment. The Commission has already announced a grant of £42.5 million towards the cost of creating 2,500 miles of high quality cycleways and pathways across the United Kingdom. Smaller, more local projects will also receive funding. For example, a further £736,000 has been awarded to Northamptonshire County Council towards a project to open up access to the countryside to the disabled.

A Shared Responsibility

Responsibility starts with individuals, families and local communities. With this in mind the remainder of this chapter describes:

- how we can encourage local initiative and voluntary action;

- our proposals to increase the involvement of rural people in more of the decisions which affect their daily lives;

- the rôle of local and national government in responding to rural needs.

LOCAL INITIATIVE AND VOLUNTARY ACTION

Self-help and independence are traditional strengths of rural communities. People in the countryside have always needed to take responsibility for looking after themselves and each other. They do not expect the Government to solve all their problems for them and they know that it is they who are generally best placed to identify their own needs and the solutions to them. In any case local decision making is likely to be more responsive to local circumstances than uniform plans. Improving the quality of life in the countryside starts with local people and local initiative.

Local Partnerships

For its part, the Government needs to be sensitive to local concerns. We aim to work in partnership with local people rather than impose top-down solutions. Developing policies in this way helps ensure that local needs are met and that resources are used in the most effective way.

Working in partnership can take many different forms and can involve a wide range of people. At one end of the spectrum, voluntary organisations, the churches and parish councils can act as a focus for local people working together. Mechanisms such as village appraisals and local housing needs surveys can help communities to define their priorities, identify what they can do to meet them and target limited resources effectively.

Local Exchange Trading System (LETS)

There are many ways of encouraging community action. One of the most original is the development of Local Exchange Trading Systems (LETS). These establish a local currency, in which people gain credits when they sell and write "cheques" when they buy. A local administration maintains records and issues statements. There is a central directory of local people involved and the services they can offer.

One of the advantages to local business is that there are no interest charges when a LETS account goes overdrawn. Normal cash can be used where it is most needed, while the local currency can be used to buy local goods and services, keeping their value within the community. Any LETS 'debt' merely represents a commitment to the rest of the community to provide goods or services in the future. Transactions with others in the LETS network may, depending on circumstances, give rise to an income tax liability.

At the other end of the spectrum, the Government encourages local authorities, TECs and local communities to work together on major projects. Programmes such as Rural Challenge and the Single Regeneration Budget Challenge Fund and European programmes such as Objective 5b and LEADER represent new opportunities for rural communities to shape their future.

Middleham, North Yorkshire - Rural Challenge Winner

In 1994, the Rural Development Commission awarded six prizes of £1 million to innovative projects in some of England's neediest rural areas. Middleham's successful Rural Challenge bid was led by the district and town councils and local race horse trainers. By working together the whole community was involved in preparing a project which sought to secure an economic future for its young people through developing training and the race horse industry, encourage tourism, provide community facilities and improve the environment. Almost a third of the project's funding will come from private sector resources, in addition to substantial funding from the European Community.

The project will improve facilities for training horses, including an all weather gallop. A new community college will help young people improve their skills to the benefit of both their long term careers and the local stables. It will also offer courses aimed at diversifying skills so that those who leave horse racing can find other employment. At the local tourist attraction of Middleham Castle, disability access will be introduced and a first floor walkway will be constructed to offer better views. It is intended to market tourist breaks which will include visits to the stables.

Middleham, North Yorkshire

Through working together, rural communities will develop the strength and vitality to improve their quality of life. This must include newcomers, commuters and second home owners who have as real a part to play as people who have lived in a village all their lives.

Rural Community Councils

Rural Community Councils (RCCs) play a valuable part in strengthening rural communities and helping local people to develop local solutions to local problems such as the closure of a village shop. RCCs coordinate voluntary work in rural areas across most of England and provide advice and support to rural communities. The Rural Development Commission (RDC) currently provides £3 million a year to help RCCs carry out their work. We particularly value RCCs' assessments of local needs, including village appraisals, housing and transport surveys and their work on village shops.

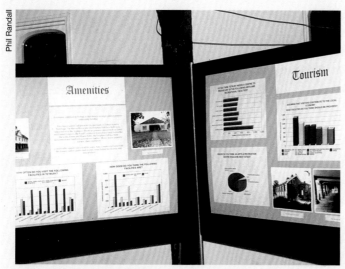

Tetbury Town Appraisal Exhibition

Tetbury Town Appraisal

Village and town appraisals offer an opportunity to canvass the opinion of local residents on a range of issues to provide a basis for future local decisions. One such appraisal was undertaken by a group of local residents in Tetbury in the Cotswolds. They sent a questionnaire to each household, and received a response rate of 60%.

The subsequent report set out residents' views on the local development plan, including proposed housing developments; traffic management, including the benefits and costs of a bypass and the location of new pedestrian crossings; health services; refuse collection; schools' class sizes, subject choice and provision for sports; and the police's presence on the beat and community liaison. The whole project, including an exhibition to publicise the report, cost just over £6,000. This was funded by the RDC, Rural Action and local people, including local businesses.

Rural Action

Rural Action stimulates local initiative by rural communities to improve their quality of life and provides over £1 million to fund small projects as diverse as pond clearing and traffic calming measures. The scheme provides expert advice, training and funding, and in return recipients contribute time and effort. Because Rural Action has been successful in stimulating new community action, we shall continue to fund the scheme for a further three years.

Country Work

Earlier this year, Action for Communities in Rural England (ACRE) and the Rural Community Councils introduced the Country Work scheme. Country Work provides grants for economic projects that improve employment prospects for rural people and actively encourage the involvement of local people and groups within rural communities. Government funding for the scheme (£370,000 over three years) is provided through the Rural Development Commission. It has been matched by pledges of support from the Post Office and British Telecom (£375,000 each over the same period).

Voluntary Action

People's willingness to help each other is an important feature of life in rural areas and is one of the great strengths of rural England, although it often goes unrecognised. The range and extent of volunteering in rural communities in England is amongst the widest in Europe. There is a long tradition of volunteering through organisations such as the Women's Institute, the Women's Royal Voluntary Service and village hall committees. This huge reservoir of talent in rural areas includes retired people with particular skills and experience.

Informal volunteering too is a feature of rural communities. Shopping for a neighbour or offering a lift to someone without transport is not just good neighbourliness but the hallmark of a thriving rural community. However:

- relatively few young people volunteer, and there is potential to involve them much more in local voluntary activities;

- rural communities may not be able to rely so heavily in the future on the contribution of women, who currently make up a high proportion of volunteers, as they are increasingly drawn into the labour market;

- in remoter areas, where people are widely dispersed, it can be more difficult to establish networks which provide advice and support for volunteers.

The types of volunteering in rural areas are also distinct from the national pattern. Rural volunteers tend to take part in a variety of activities for different organisations rather than concentrate on particular causes. Not surprisingly, two thirds of rural volunteers are involved in providing services. Recreational activities, pre-school playgroups and youth clubs also rely heavily on volunteering. In all this, transport is particularly important. Yet the rules surrounding the taxation of voluntary drivers are complicated and can cause confusion. To help volunteer drivers the Inland Revenue has produced clear guidance on how the rules operate and a simplified system for calculating whether or not there is a taxable profit element in the mileage allowance they receive.

The burden of over-regulation can fall heavily on small organisations and deter people from volunteering. We are working with the voluntary sector to identify ways in which we can avoid putting unnecessary burdens or obstacles in the way of local initiative. As well as clarifying the position on the taxation of voluntary drivers, we have also produced guidance on simplifying licence applications for village halls.

In recent years, environmental voluntary work such as repairing footpaths or monitoring bird populations has become increasingly popular. This provides an opportunity for people from towns and cities, as well as for local volunteers, to contribute to the conservation of the countryside and to improve understanding between urban and rural communities.

Make a Difference

In June 1995 the Government announced a new package to support volunteering as part of the "Make a Difference" initiative. This will help to strengthen volunteering in rural areas in a number of ways:

- Our intention is that Youth Challenge will, by the end of 1997, provide an opportunity for all young people between 15 and 25 to volunteer if they wish to do so no matter where they live;

- 20 new local volunteer development agencies will be set up by the end of 1995 in districts where there is no local agency such as a Volunteer Bureau or Council for Voluntary Service. Many of these districts are in rural areas. The Government will provide funding of up to £60,000 a year for two years for each new agency. This support for new agencies is an opportunity to encourage more volunteers in rural areas;

- the Government will provide £1.5 million for 50 innovative projects to encourage volunteering by older people and the young. We have welcomed applications for projects in rural areas. The winners will be announced in the autumn of 1995;

- the Government will ask the new Volunteering Partnership which has been set up to advise the Government on how best to promote volunteering, to take due account of volunteers in rural areas.

COMMUNITY INSTITUTIONS

Within small communities the church, the village hall and the pub are a focus for village life, a place for people to meet each other. Village shops and post offices too have a vital rôle to play.

In villages where community facilities are limited, the joint use of existing facilities such as village halls, schools, churches and health service buildings can help make best use of available resources. The Rural Development Commission is planning a number of pilot projects to test the feasibility of extending this joint use concept more widely across the countryside.

Heywood Comprehensive School

The Heywood Comprehensive School in Cinderford, Forest of Dean, is open to the public between 8.00am and 10.00pm seven days a week. The school is home to a youth club and a job club. Its facilities include meeting rooms, a keep fit centre and a sports hall run jointly with the district council. It also contains an exhibition hall, and a drama theatre and has a swimming pool.

The school building provides after school childcare facilities. Mini buses pick up children after 3.00pm or their parents drop them off. The children stay in the school until 5.30pm, during which time they can use all the facilities provided. The after school scheme is run by qualified staff trained by the district council.

Village and community halls play a particularly important rôle in small rural communities. They provide a space for entertainment and recreation, a meeting place for voluntary groups and a location for activities such as child care, over 60s clubs and youth clubs. The Government is making it easier for village halls to host a wide range of activities by simplifying licence applications. The number of licences currently required for community premises, each involving separate application and renewal procedures, imposes a significant burden on the management committees of such premises. The requirements of the different licences often overlap. As part of our deregulation initiative, it will in future be possible to apply for public entertainment, cinema and theatre licences for small premises in a single annual application. We have published guidance on this for voluntary groups and local authorities.

The Rural Development Commission provides £850,000 a year to support the improvement of village halls and community centres, as well as the provision of new halls and centres. The Commission is simplifying the administration of its assistance for village halls to make it easier for communities to apply.

The Churches

Churches continue to be a central focus of spiritual and community life in many small rural communities. They form the major voluntary organisations in much of the countryside. The report *Faith in the Countryside*, which was commissioned by the Archbishops of Canterbury and York and published in 1990, made an important contribution to our understanding of rural concerns and of the Church of England's response to them. The Churches can help to build bridges between different sections of the rural community and between town and country, and they can give a lead on the traditional values associated with rural life, such as good neighbourliness and stewardship of the land. We will discuss with the Churches ways of working more closely with them in the countryside.

Parish Councils

Parish councils have the potential to respond effectively to the needs and priorities of local people and to represent their views. The Environment Act 1995 ensures representation for parish councils on the new National Park authorities. We now intend to help parish councils develop their rôle further in a number of ways.

Nursling and Rownhams Youth Parish Council

Nursling and Rownhams Youth Parish Council was established to listen and respond to the needs of young people in their Hampshire parish. Lack of play facilities was identified as a priority for action, and within the first year they had established a new playground and had plans for two more. They also encouraged the local council to start work on a Mountain Bike Trail as well as arranging a litter awareness week which included delivering leaflets which they had designed themselves. They have received strong support from the main parish council.

Delegation and Consultation - Our 1992 consultation paper *The Rôle of Parish and Town Councils in England* proposed that principal authorities - district and county councils and unitary authorities - should be **encouraged** to delegate more of their functions to parish and town councils such as refuse collection, litter control, the maintenance of sports facilities and highways issues. It also proposed that they should be **required** to consult parish and town councils, on a far wider range of local issues than is currently the case, such as management of local facilities and local highways matters. These proposals received widespread support.

Following its review of shire counties between 1992 and 1995, the Local Government Commission concluded in its report[1] that parish and town councils should play a more important rôle as consultative and representative bodies. It recommended that a clear consultative framework should be established between parish and town councils and principal authorities which would ensure that parish and town councils had rights to the following:

- a clear statement of matters affecting the local community on which they would be consulted, with the areas for consultation being widely drawn;

- sufficient information from the principal authorities about local matters on which parish and town councils' views had been requested;

- a written explanation from the principal authority were it to disagree, as it legitimately might, with the views of the parish or town council;

- regular meetings between representatives of the principal authorities and the parish and town councils to discuss matters of common interest.

We agree that such a formal consultative framework should be put in place to underpin the relationship between principal authorities and parish and town councils. We shall introduce legislation at the earliest opportunity to provide this framework.

Given that parish and town councils vary in size and capability and in their willingness to take on additional responsibilities, it would not be right to **require** principal authorities to delegate their functions to parish and town councils. Nevertheless, we are keen to encourage delegation by means of agency agreements between authorities where these would be practicable and cost effective. In general, the consultative framework between parish and town councils and principal authorities should include a formal assessment of the functions which will be delegated to parish and town councils.

[1] *Renewing Local Government in the English Shires - A Report on the 1992-1995 Structural Review, The Local Government Commission for England March 1995. HMSO (ISBN 0117801127)*

During the debate about local government reform, county and district councils committed themselves to improving consultation and devolving powers to parish councils. **We shall be seeking a detailed account of how those promises have been kept and seeking to encourage further devolution wherever possible.** Subsidiarity is a vital component of democracy. It is not just a matter of devolution to district and parish councils but also to school governors, village hall committees and local hospital trusts. All decisions which can be made at very local level are best made there.

Rights of Way - We intend to encourage parish councils to play a more active rôle in the management of footpaths within their area. This is described in more detail in Chapter Four.

New Powers - Parish councils are well-placed to take a more active rôle in crime prevention and in community transport. These are both areas where the very local knowledge and experience of parish councils can help to deliver more responsive and effective services. **We would like to enable those parish councils which wish to do so to take on modest additional responsibilities in these areas.** Chapter Three describes our proposals in more detail under the sections on Crime and Transport.

The resources for these activities would be raised entirely through the parish council's precept on its council tax payers. Local residents would therefore have a keen interest in ensuring that the resources were well spent. **We invite comments on these proposals by March 1996**[1]. We will be discussing them in more detail with the local authority associations before we proceed to the necessary legislation.

Audit Requirements - For the smallest parish councils, audit fees can represent an excessive burden. Our consultation paper on the Accounts and Audit Regulations, issued in July 1995, announced our intention to work with the Chartered Institute of Public Finance and Accountancy to produce a statement of proper practices for parish councils. This could save parishes effort in their auditing. A further option, requiring primary legislation, would be to abolish the audit requirement for the smallest parishes altogether, subject to safeguards on accountability. **We invite views on this proposal alongside the proposals for extending parish councils powers which are outlined above.**

New Parishes - For historical reasons, parish and town councils do not exist in every part of the country. We welcome the establishment of new parishes where none currently exists. **We are reviewing current policy on setting up new parishes and, in particular, the criteria in DOE Circular 121/77**[2].

Training and Advice - The Rural Development Commission is considering ways in which it can help to enhance the rôle of parish councils and community groups. Options include training for parish councillors and support for county associations of parish councils, assisting with the provision of community workers, parish appraisals and information and advice networks.

---

[1] *Comments should be sent to Steven Watts, Rm N7/16, Department of the Environment, 2 Marsham Street, London SW1P 3EB*

[2] *Circular 121/77 - 'Local Government Act 1972 Parish Reviews' (12 December 1977)*

Cheltenham and Gloucestershire College of Higher Education

Students on the Local Policy course at the Cheltenham and Gloucester College of Higher Education

Training for Parish Clerks

Cheltenham and Gloucester College of Higher Education offers courses for parish and town clerks, councillors and others involved with local communities in the countryside. About 600 people have attended the courses since they started in 1987.

The courses, developed with the support of the Rural Development Commission, aim to provide the skills required to generate active communities, to encourage local debate and to contribute to local decision making. Each course offers a combination of home based study, local tutorial support and residential schools. Real issues facing local people, such as housing, community care, planning, environmental protection, local facilities and services are addressed together with practical modules on administration, law, finance and resources and methods of communication. For those unable to take one of the courses, a useful DIY pack entitled *Working for Your Parish* is available from the Centre for Local Policy Studies at the College.

LOCAL AND NATIONAL GOVERNMENT

It is all too easy for national and local government to overlook areas of need in the countryside. Pockets of hardship tend to be smaller and less concentrated than in cities and they can be masked by a generally affluent community and an attractive environment. County, district and unitary local authorities are the main providers of services in rural areas, and their sensitivity to the needs of rural communities can have a significant impact on the quality of life in rural areas.

Local Government

Local authorities know the local area, represent local people and have resources and powers, including planning powers, to influence change. But they too need to be alive to the concerns of other partners, of local businesses and above all local people.

Rural Strategies

To develop an integrated approach to policies affecting the countryside, local authorities can encourage the preparation of Rural Strategies, in partnership with other bodies and the local community. These provide a useful mechanism to identify rural needs and respond with flexible and targeted policies. This concept was developed and promoted in 1992 by our three countryside agencies - the Rural Development Commission, the Countryside Commission and English Nature. Since then about half of all county councils have produced Rural Strategies. The three agencies are reviewing the work done so far and will consider whether to produce further guidance on the basis of existing good practice.

Examples of Rural Strategies

Wiltshire's Rural Strategy was led by the County Council with a steering group including senior county, district and parish councillors, the Rural Development Commission and Wiltshire Rural Community Council; conservation groups including the Countryside Commission and Wiltshire Wildlife Trust; farming interests; and rural voluntary organisations. Four priorities have emerged: the provision of affordable housing, encouraging a viable rural economy, accessibility to services and maintenance of the intrinsic character of Wiltshire villages and countryside. These have now been incorporated into action plans by the agencies represented on the steering group.

In contrast, Berkshire Rural Community Strategy was led by the non-statutory Berkshire Community Council with the objective of fostering diverse and sustainable rural communities and the countryside. Those involved were drawn from the County Council, Rural Development Commission, Reading University, Council for the Protection of Rural England, the Churches, and district and parish council representatives. The strategy highlights the need for community action, information and resources, and stresses the importance of coordination, monitoring and review. Its recommendations are now being pursued by an Implementation Group. Transport is a priority issue for action, and conferences are planned next year on the rural economy and rural community care.

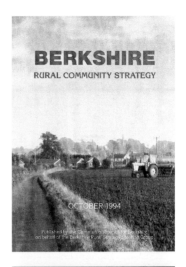

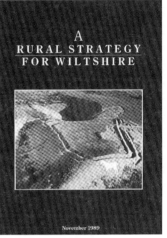

The Earth Summit in 1992 called for each local authority to adopt a Local Agenda 21 for its local community by 1996. Through Local Agenda 21 local authorities are working with businesses, voluntary organisations and community groups to identify what sustainable development means at the local level. As part of the Local Agenda 21 initiative, the Local Government Management Board has prepared guidance for local authorities with ideas on how to achieve sustainable development in rural areas.[1]

Resources for Local Government

It is national government's responsibility to ensure that local government has adequate resources to respond to the full range of local needs. The local government finance system allows for the additional cost of delivering some services in sparsely populated rural areas. This is done through the Standard Spending Assessments, which are used to calculate Revenue Support Grant for local authorities.

There is already allowance for sparsity of population for the education service and for some local authority services such as refuse collection and disposal, recreation and libraries. However, it is difficult to develop an accurate measure of the additional cost of delivering services in rural areas and we have therefore decided to undertake research to provide better information on the factors which give rise to higher costs in both sparsely and densely populated areas. This research is expected to be completed by the summer of 1996 and its findings will be published. We will discuss with the Local Authority Associations whether it is desirable and feasible to modify the Standard Spending Assessments in the light of new research findings.

---

[1] *Sustainable Development in Rural Areas, Local Agenda 21 Roundtable Guidance. The Local Government Management Board 1994*

Local government itself can generate additional spending resources by making the best use of its assets. The Government has already introduced incentives which encourage local authorities to sell under-utilised assets and which allow additional investment. We now intend to introduce special arrangements to allow county councils to re-invest the proceeds from the sale of county farms in support of rural policies.

County councils own about 5,000 agricultural smallholdings, or county farms, in England, with an open market value of up to £350 million. The original rôle of these farms was to provide a first rung on the farming ladder for new tenants but in practice, because of the very low turn-over of tenancies, only a very small number of vacancies arise each year. In addition, the Agricultural Tenancies Act 1995 is expected to lead to a significant increase in the area of land offered by private landlords for letting, including to new entrants.

Some councils have decided to retain their farms for their original purpose, perhaps having regard also to their value as a conservation or educational resource. Others, conscious of the significant amounts of capital tied up in these estates, have decided to dispose of some or all of them in order to release funds for other needs. Up to now these decisions have been taken in the light of the current requirement that local authorities must use half of the proceeds from any such sales to redeem debt.

In order to encourage all local authorities to make a balanced assessment of the future rôle, management and ownership of their farms and to develop coherent strategies for their future, **we will introduce a special scheme under the Private Finance Initiative from 1 April next year.** This will require only 10% of receipts from sales of county farms to be used to redeem debt, thus giving increased spending power to those local authorities making disposals. This special scheme will be limited to:

- sales of county farms where the sitting tenant is given the opportunity to purchase, before sale is offered to third parties; and

- transactions completed between 1 April 1996 and 31 March 1998.

Our aim is that the increased spending power made available to councils from the sale of farms should be targeted on initiatives to improve the quality of life in rural areas, in partnership with the private sector, for example by stimulating rural employment, enhancing the environment or improving local services. To encourage this, we will issue further guidance in 1996 on the types of partnership arrangements we believe should be supported. In the meantime we invite comments and suggestions on what this guidance should include[1].

National Government Response to Rural Issues

Shared responsibility for the quality of life in the countryside involves a combination of responsive national policies and local discretion. We in national government have a responsibility to ensure that our policies respond to the realities of living and working in rural areas.

---

[1] *Comments and suggestions should be sent to Bryony Houlden, P2/128, Department of the Environment, 2 Marsham Street, London SW1P 3EB*

Countryside Agencies

Our countryside agencies help safeguard the varied economic, social and environmental interests of rural areas.

The Rural Development Commission is the Government's statutory adviser on the economic and social development of rural areas in England and on the concerns of people who live and work in the countryside. We wish to see the Commission strengthen its influence on policies and public debate about the countryside and ensure that all Government Departments, and the Government Offices for the Regions, are well informed about rural concerns. This includes monitoring economic and social trends so that our policies can be based on good quality, up-to-date information. The Commission also encourages economic regeneration in priority Rural Development Areas and provides support across the countryside for a network of voluntary action and for key services such as village shops and rural transport.

The Countryside Commission advises on the conservation and enhancement of the beauty of the English countryside and the promotion of opportunities for its enjoyment by the public. The Commission has a strong record of innovation and experimentation and has worked up a number of major recent initiatives, including Countryside Stewardship, Community Forests and the Parish Paths Partnership, which have influenced the direction of rural policy. We expect the Commission to continue to fulfil this rôle and we have set the new Chairman this priority.

English Nature provides advice on wildlife conservation to Government and others including local authorities and voluntary groups. It will continue to be responsible for the establishment, maintenance and management of National Nature Reserves, the notification and conservation of Sites of Special Scientific Interest and the recommendation of Special Protection Areas under the EC Birds Directive and Special Areas of Conservation under the Habitats Directive.

We look to the three countryside agencies to work more closely together. In 1994 we examined the case for merging the Countryside Commission and English Nature but concluded that the most effective solution would be a programme of cooperative working, including on a character map of the English Countryside. We will also encourage a similar programme of joint working between the Countryside Commission and the Rural Development Commission to develop initiatives which enhance environmental quality and promote economic opportunity.

The three countryside agencies are developing closer working links with the new Government Offices for the Regions to ensure that rural concerns are fully reflected in the Government's regional programmes. For example the recently extended Objective 5b Programmes, whose primary purpose is to encourage economic regeneration in those parts of the countryside which are most in need, contain explicit provision for environmental improvement. We are therefore inviting English Nature and the Countryside Commission to work with the Government Offices in order to develop a strategic environmental dimension for these programmes. The Rural Development Commission will also continue to strengthen its working relations with the new Business Link offices, which provide advice to businesses in rural as well as urban areas.

Listening

The extensive consultation that we undertook as part of the preparations for this White Paper was not an isolated exercise. We will continue to listen and, far from being the last word, this White Paper is intended to act as a catalyst for further debate. Some of our proposals require discussion and consultation, while others will be set out more fully in documents which we shall publish shortly.

Government Offices

The ten Government Offices for the Regions were established in April 1994. They bring together the regional offices of four departments: Environment, Trade and Industry, Education and Employment and Transport. The Home Office also has a permanent presence in each office.

The Government Offices work in partnership with local people to promote competitiveness, sustainable economic development and regeneration. They have an important rôle in housing and planning, issues which are of great concern to people in rural areas.

Historically, many of the programmes they administer have had an urban focus. However, this is changing. Government Offices' involvement in programmes such as the Single Regeneration Budget which covers rural as well as urban areas, Rural Challenge and Objective 5(b) of the European Structural Funds means that their work is increasingly involved with rural areas.

The realities of rural life mean that policies cannot be dealt with in traditional, sectoral ways which, for example, consider education, housing and transport in isolation from each other. We need to be constantly alert to the rural dimension of all areas of Government policy and to the relationships between them. We will therefore introduce new mechanisms to ensure that rural concerns are properly integrated into our national and regional policies:

- we will charge our Economic, Domestic and Environment Cabinet Committee which has hitherto been restricted to consideration of environmental issues, with ensuring speedy progress in implementing the commitments made in this White Paper, and with considering the rural dimension of policies across Government;

- it is part of our philosophy that if commitments are made they should be followed through to practical action, and that progress in achieving them should be monitored and reported. We intend to apply this principle to the Rural White Paper. We shall report next year;

- the new Government Offices for the Regions will build on the success of their regional Rural White Paper seminars and will continue to meet regularly with representatives of rural communities. We will also explore ways of enabling them to work more closely with our countryside agencies, the Forestry Commission and the regional organisation of MAFF, for example by introducing new arrangements to ensure regular and effective interdepartmental coordination at regional level. The Government Offices will thus remain sensitive to rural concerns.

2. WORKING IN THE COUNTRYSIDE

INTRODUCTION

The countryside has always been a place of work. It is our firm intention that it should remain so. Rural businesses contribute to the prosperity of the nation as a whole and locally they create the jobs which sustain individual communities.

We wish therefore to see rural businesses enjoy freedom to grow and seize new opportunities. To succeed, all businesses, rural and urban alike, must develop their ability to compete effectively with businesses elsewhere in Europe and in the rest of the world. Sustainable development in the countryside must involve thriving and competitive economic activity, as many responses to the Rural White Paper consultation confirmed. Equally, rural enterprise should develop in ways which respect and enhance the environment. It is the reconciliation of these two priorities which will make sustainable development a reality.

Our overriding economic objectives for the countryside must therefore be:

- to maximise the competitiveness of rural business by creating the conditions for them to build on economic successes and by helping to stimulate new and varied forms of wealth creation;

- to do this in ways which respect the environment.

Economic Success

Traditionally, economic activity in the countryside relied heavily on land-based industries, like agriculture, mining and quarrying. There has also been significant employment in defence establishments. Since 1950 the change in all this has been dramatic. The number of workers in agriculture in the United Kingdom has fallen by well over a half, while the number of those employed in mining and quarrying has fallen by about 95%. Defence jobs have been progressively cut, particularly as a result of the ending of the Cold War. Yet despite this, the countryside is far from being in decline. Agriculture continues to thrive, and new enterprises have developed to sustain rural employment and prosperity. Manufacturing and service activities based on new technologies are more readily accommodated in a rural environment, and an improved road network and better telecommunications links have created opportunities for business development and new patterns of employment in the countryside.

Jon Stone, Rural Development Commission

A restored stable at Haltwhistle, Northumberland, provides classrooms and offices for Equistudy, who create and market educational packages for the British Horse Society examinations

This is in stark contrast to many other parts of Europe, where rural depopulation is a major concern. Here, we have a net influx of people into the countryside. Many have moved because they value the environment and many have brought additional entrepreneurial flair, technical skills and capital for investment. This is likely to continue and forecasts suggest a growth in the population of rural areas of 12% by 2025.

All this is reflected in a strong growth in employment. Between 1984 and 1991, the number of employee jobs in rural local authority districts increased by 9.2% compared with an average for England as a whole of 3%. Total employment grew twice as fast as the average for England as a whole between winter 1992/93 and winter 1994/95.

Small firms are in the vanguard. Their growth is greatest in rural areas - as is the extent of self-employment. This helps to explain why most rural areas enjoy lower levels of unemployment than other parts of the country. In 1994, 5.1% of people of working age in the countryside were unemployed, compared to 7% for England as a whole[1]. The proportion was lower than the average for England in 130 out of 148 rural local authority districts.

Situated on a Somerset farm, the Fairchild Company uses its own organic wool to make mattresses for cots to king sized beds. Winner of Country Living Small Business Award

Figure 6

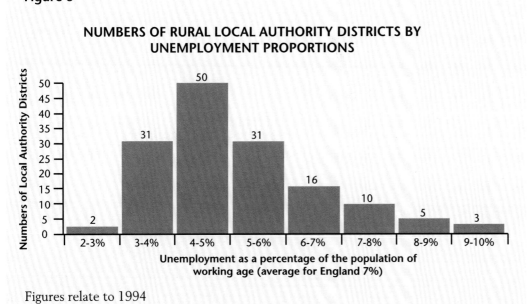

NUMBERS OF RURAL LOCAL AUTHORITY DISTRICTS BY UNEMPLOYMENT PROPORTIONS

Figures relate to 1994
Source: Department for Education and Employment

The diversification of businesses in rural areas is a strength. It means that the countryside is less vulnerable to changes affecting any one particular sector. The challenge now is for rural enterprise to build upon this success.

A National Economy

Rural businesses have never in practice been isolated from the rest of the country and recent changes have made this even more true so that patterns of employment are becoming increasingly similar across the country. In the countryside there has been a significant growth in service businesses and in new manufacturing. For example, in Great Britain in the period 1960 to 1987 there was an increase in manufacturing jobs in rural areas of 19.7% compared to an overall decline of 37.5%.

[1] *Figures are based on the claimant count.*

Nevertheless, the relative importance of different forms of employment naturally varies between areas. Figure 7 shows that the importance of manufacturing as a direct employer in rural areas is little different from that in urban areas. It also shows that even in the remoter local authority districts agriculture directly employs only about 6% of employees.

Figure 7

Economic Structure in Urban and Rural England, 1989[1]

Percentage of employees in each sector

	Metro-politan	Urban	Coalfield	Rural Accessible	Rural Remote	Total England
Other (Public) Services	30.0	29.2	25.5	28.3	26.9	29.1
Manufacturing	21.2	24.2	33.7	25.7	23.3	23.8
Distribution & Hotels	19.9	21.7	17.9	22.0	23.8	21.2
Financial & Business Services	15.6	12.3	4.6	9.3	6.2	12.4
Transport & Communications	6.9	6.1	4.2	4.9	6.0	6.2
Construction	4.5	4.3	5.4	4.9	5.3	4.6
Energy & Water	1.7	1.8	7.2	1.9	2.2	1.9
Agriculture	0.1	0.4	1.0	3.0	6.2	1.3

The area classification is based on Local Authority Districts.

Today's rural businesses trade widely across regional and international boundaries and rural enterprises tend to be less parochial in their marketing outlook than urban businesses.

Figure 8

Market Orientation of Firms in Rural and Urban Areas[2]

	Rural Remote	Rural Accessible	Urban
Locality	15.7	11.8	23.3
Region	24.8	24.2	23.0
Rest of UK	50.3	47.3	39.8
Exports	11.0	16.7	12.2

Figures show the proportion of markets of businesses in rural and urban areas accounted for by sales to different localities.
Notes:Locality <10 miles, Region 10-50 miles, rest of UK>50 miles

Yet, despite these differences, all businesses, rural as well as urban, depend equally on national policies to achieve economic stability, low inflation and low interest rates. The 1995 White Paper on Competitiveness[3] set out in detail what the Government is doing to enhance the competitive position of the United Kingdom as a whole. Although improving competitiveness is primarily a matter for business itself, the Government also has an important role.

[1] *The Economy of Rural England by R Tarling, J Rhodes, J North and G Broom Rural Development Commission 1993 [ISBN 1 869964 35 7]*
[2] *Business Success in the Countryside: the Performance of Rural Enterprise by D Keeble, P Tyler, G Broom and J Lewis Department of the Environment 1992. [HMSO] [ISBN 0 11 752663 0]*
[3] *Competitiveness : Forging Ahead, Department of Trade and Industry 1995 [1995] [HMSO] [ISBN 0 10 128672 4]*

To facilitate enterprise and help business become internationally competitive, we shall continue to:

- create the framework in which companies can prosper - maintaining low inflation and sound public finances, making markets work more efficiently, removing unnecessary regulatory burdens, raising standards in education and training, ensuring efficient communication and transport infrastructure;

- help companies to help themselves - spreading best practice, sponsorship of business' needs, and where necessary, providing direct assistance, particularly for smaller firms, and investing in science and technology research[1].

Diversity of Success

The 1995 White Paper on Competitiveness committed us to exploring how best to ensure that rural areas make an increasing contribution to national competitiveness. The countryside's economic success is not uniform. Inequalities, often masked by surrounding affluence or by the attractiveness of the environment, demand sensitivity to the economic differences between one part of the countryside and another, if everyone in the countryside is to have opportunities to enjoy a reasonable standard of living.

Not least must we recognise the significant differences between small firms in remoter and more inaccessible parts of the countryside and those close to urban centres. The former tend to experience more constraints on business development and efficiency. For example, they may experience a shortage of skilled and technical workers and of managerial and professional staff and can be disadvantaged by their distance from customers and suppliers. They may also have inferior transport and telecommunications links compared with firms closer to large centres. This makes it harder for them to mirror the healthy growth that looks set to continue in rural businesses closer to towns.

There are other issues too of which we must be aware which affect all rural enterprises to some extent. The uptake of business support services and training is often lower. Partly this is because rural businesses, their workforces and the rural unemployed are located further away from training providers than their urban counterparts, and limited public transport hinders access. But it is also because small businesses are less likely than large ones to be able to provide in-house training or to be able to afford to release staff for external training.

There are also particular places which have faced more difficulties than others because of fundamental change in an economic sector on which they relied heavily in the past. Rural collieries now employ only 5,500 people, compared with over 60,000 ten years ago. In Cornwall, extraction of china clay employs a third fewer people than 20 years ago, and tin mining has almost ceased. Even in a growth business like tourism, change has not universally benefited rural areas. Small seaside towns suffer now that the main holiday at the seaside is less popular than it once was and they face stiff competition from resorts overseas.

Not all of these places have been able to diversify rapidly enough to compensate for such major changes. In some, unemployment is, as we have shown, above the national average. In others, aggregate statistics may understate the unemployment problems faced by certain groups. That is why the Government recognises, through the system of designations, those rural areas which suffer from a concentration of economic and social problems.

[1] *The 1995 Forward Look of Government-funded Science, Engineering and Technology [HMSO] provides a comprehensive statement of the Government's strategy for publicly funded science, engineering and technology.*

Such designations enable us to assist rural areas and enterprises to meet these challenges. In addition to pursuing wider economic policies which will help all parts of the countryside to grow and prosper, we shall:

- use targeted national and European regeneration programmes to help areas with particular needs;

- work with local economic partners to ensure that our programmes are tailored to meet locally defined priorities.

Economic Development and the Environment

In seeking new jobs we must not forget that the appeal of the English countryside is central to its economic prosperity. It is therefore particularly important to ensure that the environment is not damaged by the process of economic development. Many rural businesses regard a pleasant working environment as one of the benefits of their location and one of the reasons why they moved there. Rural tourism too relies heavily for its success on the attractiveness of the rural environment and is estimated to account for expenditure of about £8 billion a year and to sustain about 400,000 jobs in England.

With this in mind, we shall:

- continue to shape planning policies so as to enable development to take place in ways which protect and, where possible, enhance the environment;

- further promote the sensitive location and design of new development.

This derelict building was redeveloped for the Lithgill Dale Skill Centre, Manor Farm, Bakewell, Derbyshire

Jon Stone/Rural Development Commission

FRAMEWORK FOR ENTERPRISE

Planning

The planning system guides the development and use of land in the public interest. It reconciles the needs of development and conservation, and secures economy, efficiency and amenity in the use of land. By integrating the twin objectives of development and environmental protection, the planning system contributes to sustainable development.

Our planning policies for the countryside are set out in Planning Policy Guidance note 7, *The Countryside and the Rural Economy* (PPG 7). This emphasises the importance of economic diversification and the need to accommodate change, while continuing to conserve the countryside. PPG7 stresses that rural areas can accommodate many forms of development if they are sensitively designed and located.

We will shortly publish a guide for local planning authorities to promote good practice in planning for rural diversification. This will advise local planning authorities to:

- assess the needs and opportunities for diversification in their areas, in co-operation with Government Departments, the Rural Development Commission and local bodies such as Training and Enterprise Councils, so as to help the preparation of positive planning policies;

- co-operate with local bodies to compile and promote registers of rural buildings with unimplemented planning permission for economic re-use;

- inform unsuccessful applicants for planning permission what forms of development are acceptable under the development plan;

- recognise the economic potential of projects which add value to local produce, such as processing food from one or more farms;

- integrate policies for rural diversification and environmental protection.

While rural employment needs to diversify into new ventures, local authorities are sometimes reluctant to grant planning permission for new business uses which they fear may intensify beyond what is appropriate for a rural location. One answer might be to introduce a new rural business use class which would be subject to limitations on the traffic generated. By helping to reduce the risk of uncontrolled expansion, this could give local authorities more confidence in allowing enterprise to diversify. **We will shortly issue a consultation paper on how this new use class might work in practice.**

We wish to have planning appeals, including those for small rural developments, dealt with quickly. **We will issue a Circular before the end of 1995 to help achieve this and make the process more user friendly, under existing powers and procedures.**

We will issue a draft revision of PPG7 for public consultation, drawing on research to be published later this year. Among other things, we will propose allowing greater discrimination in favour of re-use of rural buildings for business rather than residential purposes.

A number of responses to the Rural White Paper consultation questioned the relationship between PPG7 and PPG13, *Transport*. PPG13 seeks to reduce the need to travel by influencing the location of development in relation to transport provision and supporting developments which encourage walking, cycling and public transport use. We recognise that there is less scope for reducing reliance on the private car in rural areas than in the town. PPG13 means that in rural areas the main focus of development is on those existing centres where employment, housing and other facilities can be provided close together. This promotes sustainable development by strengthening villages and market towns, protecting the open countryside and reducing the need to travel. The re-use of rural buildings, which can encourage rural enterprise and jobs, should not lead to further dispersal of activity on such a scale as to prejudice town and village vitality.

We discuss our policies for dealing with the pressures of development on the rural environment in Chapter Four.

Rural Business Unit

One idea that has been put to us is that commercial activities associated with a rural estate whose predominant activity is husbandry should be assessed as a single trading unit for income tax, capital gains tax and inheritance tax purposes. Under this concept of a Rural Business Unit, income from commercial activities traditionally associated with a rural estate, together with evolving diversified activities, would be treated as trading income. Relevant activities would be eligible for business property relief from inheritance tax and for capital gains tax reliefs. We are considering this case.

Deregulation

Removing unnecessary barriers to entrepreneurial activity and innovation benefits all businesses and we are committed to repealing or simplifying unnecessary regulations and administrative requirements. For example, we have:

- raised the threshold for VAT registration and deregistration to remove the burden of VAT accounting on approximately 75,000 small businesses;

- consulted on proposals to streamline the licensing of red meat slaughterhouses, to revoke outdated requirements to display signs and remove other restrictions.

We aim to ensure that, where regulations are necessary, we keep to a minimum the burdens on businesses, particularly small businesses. For example, we have worked closely with our European partners to negotiate less restrictive EC regulations on food hygiene. We are promoting a common sense approach to the enforcement of these regulations which will minimise the burdens on small producers of traditional local products.

We also aim to ensure that the law is clear. Businesses need to be able to understand exactly what is required of them. To this end, we have commissioned a study, which we expect to lead to a pilot project, for a computer-based information service to help new businesses understand their regulatory and licensing obligations. This will be of particular benefit to small businesses in rural areas.

Agricultural Tenancy Legislation

The Agricultural Tenancies Act 1995 came into force on 1 September 1995. Its purpose is to remove complex and unnecessary legal constraints on the agriculture industry. Landlords and tenants entering into new tenancies are now able to agree farm business tenancies which reflect their own particular needs. They now have more scope to agree arrangements for allowing tenants to diversify their businesses.

The reforms are intended to encourage landowners to offer a significant amount of extra land for rent. This will widen the opportunities for young people to gain a foothold in the farming industry. Established farmers will be better able to develop their existing businesses. The changes will restore confidence in the tenanted sector and enable the industry to respond better to market and policy changes.

In line with our initiatives on enforcement[1], we look to enforcement agencies in rural areas to carry out their duties with fairness, consistency and proportionality and to work constructively with rural businesses. They should apply derogations for smaller businesses sensitively in accordance with relevant guidance, and with a constant recognition that lively and innovative business is vital to rural employment. They must seek always to avoid unnecessary restrictions and instead find ways to help companies operate more efficiently. They must adopt an attitude which seeks to say 'yes' and where restriction is necessary they must always try to find a sensible and economic alternative.

To protect businesses from over-zealous enforcement we have given them rights to:

- a written explanation from the enforcement officer of any action required;

- make representations before any formal enforcement action is taken;

- an explanation of rights of appeal against enforcement decisions.

We are also promoting Local Business Partnerships to improve communications between businesses and local government enforcement agencies. These are a popular and successful way of ensuring that enforcement agencies understand the real needs and priorities of businesses.

Business Support Services

Training and business advice are important for the success of businesses in rural areas and we are taking steps to make them more widely available. The merger of the Employment and Education Departments will mean better coordination of policies to improve skill levels and promote business success.

Training and Enterprise Councils (TECs) are private companies set up to manage the provision of support for new businesses and for employer investment in training, as well as training for young people and unemployed adults. TECs play an important strategic rôle working with other bodies such as local authorities and the Rural Development Commission to agree actions for the regeneration and economic development of their local areas.

Yet small businesses may find it difficult to identify training needs and allow staff time for training, and access to a TEC's services is more difficult for businesses in remote locations. Through our strategic guidance, we encourage TECs to respond to the needs of rural businesses when developing their programmes.

Collective Enterprise Ltd

New Horizons Training Programme for Women at the Eccles House Telebusiness Centre in the Peak District National Park. The course is available free with the support of the Stockport and High Peak and North Derbyshire TECs, the European Social Fund and the Rural Development Commission. The Grade Two farmhouse and outbuildings were restored as a Business Telecottage, which is managed by Collective Enterprises Ltd, providing computers and other IT facilities, advice and training for the self-employed, small businesses and those wishing to upgrade their skills. The Centre has seen the creation of over 50 new full and part time jobs

---

[1] These include the Code for Enforcement Agencies; the powers in section 5 of the Deregulation and Contracting Out Act, 1994 to improve enforcement procedures; and the model appeals mechanism in section 6 of the same Act.

Skills Build 2000

North Derbyshire TEC is offering specialised training for ex-miners based in their local communities. Its Skills Build 2000 programme offers guidance on returning to the labour market and training, which is linked to the needs of local employers. The project provides a model for areas similarly affected by closure of mines and, more generally, for towns and villages which depend heavily on a single employer or industry

Parish Business Ambassadors

Cumbria TEC, in partnership with Voluntary Action Cumbria, is creating a network of Parish Business Ambassadors across the county. Parish Business Ambassadors, who serve on the local parish council, are people with experience of industry, agriculture or training. They can direct businesses and individuals to the various sources of public funds for economic development, carry out economic assessments of their areas and recommend ways in which parish and town councils can stimulate economic activity.

Many of the TECs' recent initiatives have focused on small businesses and improved the effectiveness of their services to rural businesses and individuals:

- the Consortium of Rural TECs (CORT) was established in 1991 as a voluntary association of rural TECs to promote training and enterprise in rural areas, and to disseminate good practice to its members;

Lincolnshire TEC operates two Countryside Job Buses as mobile job and training centres. They take advice, training and up to the minute job vacancy information out into rural areas

- Modern Apprenticeships aim to help improve competitiveness by meeting the need for higher vocational skills and promise to play an influential rôle in the development of rural industries. TECs are being asked to ensure that all young people and employers can secure access to the full range of Apprenticeships. Demand for Apprenticeships in rural areas may be low in numerical terms. In some cases therefore, TECs will need to work together to ensure adequate access to training opportunities across TEC boundaries;

- since April 1995 every TEC has delivered "Skills for Small Businesses", a new initiative funded by the Department for Education and Employment, to help small businesses to develop their in-house capacity to train. In the first year TECs will have £9 million to support the development of key workers in about 3,500 businesses. The programme will expand to cover about 24,000 businesses by 1998;

- the 1995 Competitiveness White Paper announced a new initiative to encourage small companies to work together to find shared solutions to common training needs, now called Skills Challenge, in which TECs will play a leading part;

- TECs are utilising new technology to deliver training in remote areas, for example through distance learning and teleworking;

- the "Investors in People" initiative encourages employers large and small to invest effectively in the skills needed for business success, which is central to improved business performance. It is a national standard, delivered locally through TECs, which links training and development to business objectives. In July 1995, over 14,500 small firms had made a commitment to Investors in People and 1,600 had achieved the standard.

Centre for the Application of Information Technologies for Land Based Industries

Suffolk TEC, Suffolk College and Otley College are creating an IT Centre of Excellence to help East Anglian land based industries to be more competitive in world markets. The project aims to improve local training infrastructure, overcome problems of access and introduce rural businesses to the latest information technology. New methods of training will be developed, including the use of multimedia and distance learning.

Because there are many sources of education, training and advice for businesses in rural areas, businesses can be confused about what is best for them and how to access it. This can be a particular problem for small rural businesses which cannot invest the time and resources needed to research all available opportunities.

We therefore attach special importance to the development of **Business Links** in rural areas to provide one stop shops for businesses in need of training, advice, information and support. Business Links are based on partnerships involving TECs, local authorities and other economic development agencies. In order to ensure that Business Links are sensitive to the needs of rural businesses, the Rural Development Commission is usually a Business Link partner in rural areas.

The Ministry of Agriculture, Fisheries and Food (MAFF) is conducting a pilot project to establish how best Business Links and MAFF can provide a service by which each can "signpost" each other's services to rural businesses.

Business Links are open to all businesses, whatever their size or location. Rural businesses will be able to benefit from the full range of services available through their local Business Links and local flexibility will ensure that services are targeted at specific local needs.

We aim to see 200 Business Links set up in England by the end of 1995. Every rural area will be served by its own Business Link and, by pursuing a number of initiatives focusing on the "Information Superhighway", Business Links are ensuring that even the most rural businesses can benefit from their services. All Business Links will be able to communicate directly with businesses through an electronic-mail link. In addition, the Department of Trade and Industry is embarking on a project to put Business Links on a managed version of the Internet, which will enable rural businesses to identify Business Link services, communicate with Personal Business Advisers and, ultimately, access services. Individual Business Links are pursuing the use of the Internet as an information source and a communications medium. They are also piloting the use of multimedia. Businesses coming into a Business Link could in future be linked up with the Government Offices, overseas posts and centres of expertise.

Business Link Shropshire

Business Link Shropshire covers the predominantly rural county of Shropshire

Treasure and Sons Ltd have been based in Shropshire over 200 years and in the market town of Ludlow for over 50 years. The company had seen itself as a local family firm of specialist builders. But it needed to restructure and approached BL Shropshire for advice and guidance on how to improve profitability. Kerry Thomas, BL Shropshire Personal Business Adviser, was assigned to the company and worked with the Directors to set company goals for the 21st century.

Chairman and Directors now predict a bright future for the family business and identify the following key features as critical to its turn round:

- seeing the company as a national leader in conservation and restoration work. Current work includes a building to house the Mappa Mundi and Chained Library at Hereford Cathedral and works at Warwick Castle;

- development of the craft-based skilled workforce and blending of the traditional and the 'hi-tech' skills required to undertake modern restoration work;

- a nation-wide expansion programme focusing the company on its specialist niche market;

- the support and advice from BL Shropshire, which provided the initial impetus for the review and restructuring. This helped the company to focus its activities and to become truly competitive.

The 1995 Competitiveness White Paper announced a series of further initiatives aimed at small businesses. This new package of support involves further commitments of £200 million (of which £125 million is additional public expenditure).

National Rural Education and Training Strategy Group

The Government and other agencies provide funding to underpin the work of the National Rural Education and Training Strategy Group (NRETS). This group provides a discussion forum for further and higher education interests, key representatives from training organisations, and Government agencies and departments with an involvement in rural education and training. NRETS is currently carrying out research into whether the needs of rural businesses are being fully met, and the effectiveness of the present arrangements for delivering them. This work should also provide analysis and guidance on best practice for local provision of information, training and advice for rural businesses. By working together with bodies such as NRETS, we are able to develop a clearer understanding of how to make support for small rural businesses more effective.

Uptake of Employment

Through the services provided by the Employment Service and by facilitating the provision of childcare, we help people to take up the employment opportunities that exist in rural areas.

The Employment Service (ES) is a national service which seeks to meet the needs of all its clients, whether they live in the town or the countryside, and jobseekers living in rural areas need access to it as much as those who live in towns.

ES has more offices in rural locations than any other central government organisation. Even so, some clients may live some distance away from their nearest Jobcentre. ES is continually looking for ways to improve its service in rural areas and disseminates good practice for service delivery in rural areas to its local offices. Rural jobseekers may find the following arrangements useful:

- rural clients who cannot easily reach their nearest Jobcentre can have their advisory interviews conducted by telephone. Where a frequent public transport service is not available, appointments for six-monthly restart interviews can be booked to take account of bus or train times. For rural clients who would otherwise have to travel very long distances, meetings can be arranged in a more local village hall or another convenient location;

- clients who live six or more miles from their nearest ES office can sign on fortnightly for benefits by post. Those living more than ten miles away may also make their initial claim by post. Help with bus fares is provided when postal clients attend their local office for their quarterly reviews;

- ES has set up rural Jobclubs. A fares provision enables members to travel to a Jobclub in a different town to that in which their Jobclub is based, thus widening their area of job search.

Contact Plus

This Freephone facility makes Jobcentre services and details of ES programmes available to clients in Beccles, Diss, Leiston and neighbouring villages in rural parts of Norfolk and Suffolk. ES, the Rural Development Commission (RDC), Norfolk and Waveney TEC, Waveney District Council and Mid-Suffolk District Council jointly fund the service, which attracted 2,500 calls during 1994/95.

The provision of **childcare** can be crucial in enabling parents to take up employment opportunities. However, childcare facilities in sparsely populated parts of the countryside may be scarce and may rely on volunteers even more than in the towns.

We are taking steps to increase childcare provision for school age children by creating up to 50,000 out-of-school childcare places and many of these will be in rural areas. We are also supporting:

- a "Childcare Enterprise Training Programme", developed jointly with the Consortium of Rural TECs. This will provide a flexible means by which individuals who wish to run a rural childcare enterprise and gain a National Vocational Qualification can obtain training;

St Christopher's Nursery School, Totnes, situated in a former milking parlour and farm storage area, was converted with support from a Redundant Building Grant from the RDC

Clare Pawley Rural Development Commission

Patricia French/Dimson's Kids Club

Dimsons Kids Club, Gunnislake, Cornwall is an extension of a private day nursery. It received assistance from the Devon and Cornwall Playlines Partnership, which consists of the local TEC, both the county and community councils from Devon and Cornwall, the Childminders' Association and the Rural Development Commission. It offers advice and training both on childminding and business skills. The Kids Club offers traditional rural activities, such as feeding and caring for animals, riding and craft work.

ENGLISH
PARTNERSHIPS

- a rural childcare initiative, which the RDC has been running since 1992 to raise awareness of rural childcare needs and to demonstrate ways of meeting them. The Department of Health and the RDC are funding a Rural Childcare Adviser post based in the voluntary sector. Among other functions, this post will be responsible for setting up demonstration projects to test ways of developing new services.

Childcare vouchers in Leicestershire

North West Leicestershire is an area where traditional male employment is declining and female employment increasing. Limited and expensive childcare facilities have been identified as barriers to women undertaking training and employment. The RDC, Leicestershire County Council and Leicestershire TEC jointly fund a childcare voucher scheme. This enables parents to choose which type of childcare they wish to use: a child minder, day nursery or crèche.

GOVERNMENT AND EUROPEAN PROGRAMMES

Nationwide Government Programmes

The Government has a rôle as an enabler in stimulating rural development and enterprise, against the backdrop of a strong, competitive national economy. This is done in a number of ways. National education, training, law and order and social services policies are all geared to address the needs and priorities of rural areas. We aim to ensure that taxpayers' money is used to good effect, that Government programmes work with the grain of the economies of rural areas and reflect what local communities want.

The Government also has a part to play in the regeneration of run down areas and the development of new enterprises. This means supporting individual projects and businesses in rural areas where the decline has been marked. As a result, a range of direct initiatives has been developed to complement national programmes. They include initiatives supported by the Rural Development Commission, English Partnerships, Regional Selective Assistance, European Community Structural Funds and the Single Regeneration Budget. Each of these programmes, which are described further below, aims to unlock local initiative and engage local people.

The Single Regeneration Budget (SRB) is the Government's main instrument for encouraging local regeneration. In the first round of the SRB Challenge Fund, about 40 schemes which will have an impact on rural areas have been approved. They will draw in some £40 million in Challenge Fund support with complementary private and other public investment. These schemes started from April 1995. Bids submitted for a second round are now being considered.

In addition to the SRB, there are two sources of public funds which are designed to give added help to particular areas adversely affected by rapid economic change. The first is Regional Selective Assistance (RSA) which is working in Cornwall, Cambridgeshire and Kent and many other parts of the country to create and safeguard jobs through support for projects which contribute to national and local competitiveness.

Single Regeneration Budget: The West Cornwall Initiative

The West Cornwall Initiative involves three district councils, Cornwall County Council, Devon and Cornwall TEC, English Partnerships, Barclays Bank, British Telecom and Business-in-the-Community and other agencies. Kerrier District Council acts as the lead partner.

The Initiative aims to regenerate the corridor stretching from Penzance through Hayle, Camborne and Redruth, to Falmouth and Penryn. This will involve revitalising the centres of the small towns in the area, reclaiming areas of derelict land, much of which results from 19th century tin mining, and creating new job opportunities throughout West Cornwall.

The scheme has been allocated £2.8 million for its four year span. £400,000 will be made available for the first year (1995/96). The project is expected to attract other contributions, from the public and private sectors, of £21.3 million.

The second source is the EC Structural Funds, which are targeted on a similar basis. The funds contribute to economic development, the provision of infrastructure, tourism and business support schemes, as well as training measures and local environmental improvements linked to economic regeneration.

EC Structural Funds

Two programmes within the EC Structural Funds are specifically targeted at rural areas - Objective 5(b) and LEADER II.

Objective 5(b)

Under Objective 5(b) of the Structural Funds specific rural areas receive help to improve their development and structural adjustment. The total area covered has been increased significantly. During the five year period up to 1993, the only parts of England designated to receive funds were Devon and Cornwall. We have now secured designation for six English areas for the period up to 1999, covering more than 1.7 million people. The amount available for 1994/99, about £410 million, is a substantial increase over the expenditure for 1988/93 of £66 million.

In order to attract funding, projects must include one or more of a number of specified objectives. These include support and assistance for businesses, agricultural and fishery diversification, development of tourism and cultural activities, and conservation and enhancement of the environment.

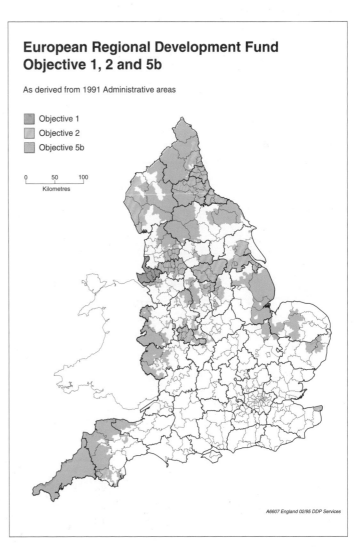

European Regional Development Fund Objective 1, 2 and 5b

As derived from 1991 Administrative areas

- Objective 1
- Objective 2
- Objective 5b

0   50   100
Kilometres

A6607 England 02/95 DDP Services

Partnership is a key feature of the operation of the programme in each area. We drew up each programme in consultation with local authorities and local organisations. Implementation closely involves Government Departments and Agencies, the European Commission and a wide range of local organisations, including local authorities, TECs, higher and further education sectors, environmental bodies and the private and voluntary sectors.

Objective 5(b) programmes complement the funding available to rural areas from other sources, including the Rural Development Commission programmes, Rural Challenge and the private sector. Support from Objective 5(b) means that many of these schemes can be extended or enhanced.

Structural Funds grants under Objective 5(b) can only cover part of the cost of a project, normally up to a half. The remainder has to be found by the applicant. Matching funding can come from a variety of sources including Government programmes, local authorities and other public bodies, TECs and the voluntary and private sectors. We have introduced new guidelines to enable private initiative and finance to make a greater contribution to the programmes. Some organisations, particularly small rural organisations with limited resources, may find it difficult to fund contributions in cash. We are pressing the European Commission to clarify their position on the sorts of contribution in kind which may be accepted as matching funding, such as the donation of land and buildings or legal or financial advice given free of charge.

Bishop Auckland College

Bishop Auckland College has received grant under the Northern Uplands Objective 5(b) programme so that it can offer improved access to skills training. The training will focus on growth areas, such as information technology and tourism, and areas of skill shortage, for example management skills. The project, which has financial backing from the Rural Development Commission (RDC), will provide premises and equipment for the delivery of vocational training, guidance and counselling. It is intended to benefit local communities whose access to such facilities is limited.

West Devon District Council

West Devon District Council, in collaboration with the RDC, has secured grant to provide infrastructure on 3 hectares of industrial land within a disused quarry near Tavistock as part of the South West Objective 5(b) programme. Completion of this project is expected to open the way for the creation of some 150 permanent jobs based on the site.

LEADER II

This programme complements the Objective 5(b) programmes. It will be targeted mainly at Objective 5(b) areas but 10% of the allocated funds may be used in bordering areas. We have obtained about £21 million in EC grant for England in 1994/99, compared with £1.2 million for 1992/94. LEADER II projects are intended above all to be innovative and to promote the acquisition of skills, initiatives by local groups which can serve as models for groups elsewhere, and other forms of rural innovation.

Rural Government Programmes

Rural Development Commission

Through the Rural Development Commission (RDC) we provide resources specifically to assist people in rural England. The regeneration of rural areas is a major aspect of the RDC's remit. The bulk of the RDC's expenditure, over £22 million, is targeted at Rural Development Areas, those areas of rural England which have participated least in the countryside's economic success. A wide range of support is available in these areas to fund integrated rural development programmes put together by local partnerships. These are designed to strengthen communities, help disadvantaged groups and lay the foundations for economic success. In addition, the RDC helps small businesses to expand by providing a package of loans, business advice and grants to convert redundant buildings into workspace.

In 1994, the RDC introduced Rural Challenge, a competition designed to stimulate the formation of innovative new partnerships which will make a significant impact on economic and social problems in Rural Development Areas. Six prizes of £1 million, to be spent over three years, are awarded each year. Local partnerships need to demonstrate that their bid will address key local problems. We will evaluate the success of **Rural Challenge** in 1997/98 and will consider whether competitive approaches should be extended to other RDC expenditure.

RURAL DEVELOPMENT AREAS

1994 Rural Challenge winner: Boughton Pumping Station

Boughton Pumping Station is one mile outside the Nottinghamshire villages of Ollerton and Boughton, which have a joint population of 12,500. The recent decline of the coal industry has had a severe effect on the area, and about 5,000 jobs have been lost since 1991.

A broad partnership involving public, private and voluntary bodies, working with the local community, came together to help regenerate the area. Their project aims to benefit the local villages through a package of business, training and community projects. It will restore the Blackburn Engine House, an Edwardian Grade II listed building, and create within it craft workshops, offices, workspace and recreational facilities for local people and visitors. The building will adopt best practice in energy efficiency and will provide a focus for initiatives and exhibitions related to renewable energy and energy efficiency. In addition the project will provide a base for training disadvantaged adults and will provide help and advice for elderly people on home security. Rural Challenge funding of £1 million will attract investment of £2.5 million from other sources.

Boughton Pumping Station, Nottinghamshire

Lincolnshire Training and Enterprise Council

Manor Upholstery , North Witham, Grantham, set up their business in 1992 with the support of Lincolnshire TEC

Business Start Up

People are more likely to start up businesses in rural areas than in cities. Some 1,148,000 new businesses started up in England in the three years up to the end of 1994[1]. Some 60,000 business start ups will be supported across England over the next seven years under the SRB Challenge Fund.

Figure 9

Differences in New Firm Formation Rates Between Urban and Rural Areas, 1980-1990[2]

	Mean new firm formation rates
Conurbations	64.4
More urbanised counties	76.7
Less urbanised counties	83.3
Rural counties	83.2

Rates are of new VAT business registrations per 1000 of the civilian labour force 1981.

We wish further to encourage self-employment in rural areas and are evaluating possible new arrangements to encourage business start ups.

Rowan Start Up Fund

This is available from Northumberland TEC's Business Advice Centres sited in locations around the county. It is aimed at those setting up new, small enterprises in Northumberland and provides financial help and a comprehensive range of advice. Businesses supported so far include driving instructors, plumbers, gardeners and a shop stocking environmentally friendly products.

Food Marketing and Sponsorship

Good marketing is essential for the agriculture, horticulture and food industries. For an increasing number of farmers and growers the principal customers are the supermarket chains. Others are finding niche markets for speciality products. The major buyers demand high product quality and consistency throughout the year. Many agriculture and food businesses are poorly organised to take advantage of the opportunities which face them. This is particularly the case among small and medium-sized companies. The food trade gap, although declining appreciably in real terms, stands at about £6 billion annually. This underlines the perennial need for British businesses continually to improve their competitiveness and market orientation.

We have developed a number of measures to help farmers add value to what they produce and to tailor their product to customer requirements, and also to help British food companies compete still more effectively in home and export markets. Our food marketing initiatives put the emphasis on helping the industry to help itself:

[1] *Source: Barclays Bank Economics Department.*
[2] *Enterprising Behaviour and the Urban-Rural Shift, D Keeble and P Tyler in Urban Studies, Vol 32, No 6 [Carfax Publishing Company for the University of Glasgow,] June 1995 ISSN 0042-0980/95/0600 975-23*

- The Ministry of Agriculture, Fisheries and Food (MAFF) has established a Market Task Force in order to find ways of encouraging individual businesses and industry sectors to strengthen their performance;

- the Processing and Marketing Grant provides capital grants for buildings and equipment. It was comprehensively reviewed in 1994 to strengthen administration and simplify procedures for applicants. In the first nine months of 1995, 78 businesses in England were awarded grants totalling £16 million;

- the Marketing Development Scheme provides flexible assistance to improve marketing and management. Grants for items such as feasibility studies and employment of key staff are available to farmers, groups and smaller food processors. The annual budget is £2.4 million. Around 150 businesses have been assisted so far.

Tinsley Foods Ltd

Tinsley Foods is a private company based in rural South Lincolnshire, which manufactures chilled foods including fresh produce, sandwiches, recipe dishes and ready-to-eat salads. Its expansion has been backed by a close partnership with leading retailers, especially Marks & Spencer.

The company is largely owned by the Tinsley family who have been farmers in Lincolnshire for 200 years. Over the last 25 years it has grown from a straightforward farming business into value-added food production, and is now one of the largest employers in the county.

With the aid of a Processing and Marketing Grant from MAFF in 1992, it built a new factory providing state-of-the-art facilities for prepared salads and vegetables. This created 100 new jobs, taking the total workforce to over 1500.

Food from Britain (FFB) is the Government's lead agency providing a comprehensive consultancy service to United Kingdom food exporters. Supported jointly by the Agriculture Departments and the food industry, it puts food exporters in direct contact with overseas customers in other European countries, North America and Japan. **Now we shall look at expanding its coverage into the Middle East.**

Together with FFB, MAFF supports innovative speciality food producers who do so much to keep alive our traditional foods and can be important employers locally. The object is to help them develop and expand, with advice on promotion, quality control, training, food safety and other statutory matters, delivered through Government assisted local Speciality Food Groups.

Leading customers are sourcing from the United Kingdom wherever possible, and British suppliers are responding to their demands. The Government will continue to help through its food sponsorship programme and ensure that help is targeted where it can achieve the best effect.

Taste of the West

Taste of the West is one of several Speciality Food Groups set up with MAFF and FFB support. It provides support to speciality food producers in the seven South Western counties. Its Guide listing members and their products is circulated to 4,000 businesses.

One of Taste of the West's principal functions is to hold trade exhibitions which act as a platform to promote members' products. The first exhibition, in November 1991, attracted 60 exhibitors and 300 trade buyers. Some 900 trade buyers attended the most recent show in March 1995.

Taste of the West's future plans include a rigorous quality management scheme for members, promotion of regional cuisine with local caterers and further "Meet the Buyer" events with national supermarket and catering companies.

MAFF also spends around £3 million a year on improving food technology. This includes support for regional Technology Transfer Centres in Shropshire, Devon and North East Lincolnshire.

FACING UP TO CHANGE

Agriculture

Traditionally, farming employed the land and the people of rural England. It was a source of wealth and position; it sustained the village community, maintained its church and fed the nation. It is still a great industry and still employs the land but the farmer's rôle as an employer of labour has diminished. Today, he takes his place with others in supporting the community, and in feeding the nation he competes with the rest of the world. Yet his response to change will be a key factor in the evolution of the countryside. As landowner, land user and seven day a week resident he will have an importance well beyond his more limited impact as direct employer.

Productivity Growth and Structural Trends

The last 50 years have seen unprecedented growth in the productivity and output of British agriculture, brought about through sustained effort on the part of many thousands of individuals, coupled with a willingness to innovate in search of best practice and to apply enthusiastically the results of scientific research. All this against a background of continued public support - first through deficiency payments and then through the Common Agricultural Policy (CAP) - which gave continuous impetus to production. In addition Government has funded research and development and advisory services to improve efficiency. The total cost of CAP to the taxpayer and other spending on agriculture in the United Kingdom in 1995/96 is around £4 billion. Since 1973, the volume of United Kingdom production has increased by around a fifth, despite the introduction of quotas in a number of sectors.

Figure 10

Comparison of UK Yields 1973-94

	1973	1994
Wheat (tonnes/hectare)	4.37	7.35
Barley (tonnes/hectare)	3.97	5.37
Oilseed rape (tonnes/hectare)	2.30	2.55
Milk (litres/cow)	3975	5372

Source: MAFF

Since 1973, in England, the total agricultural labour force has fallen by a quarter, with a particularly sharp drop in family labour and hired labour. The number of part-time workers has declined much less rapidly than full-time workers. Only 1.8% of the English labour force is currently employed in agriculture, although this figure conceals substantial local variations - in certain parishes in Devon, North Yorkshire and Shropshire more than one in five of the workforce is still in agriculture.

Figure 11

Labour Force on Agricultural Holdings in England ('000s)

	1973	1994	Change 1973/1994
Total labour force	n.a.	430.9	n.a.
Total labour force excl spouses	517.5	381.7	-26%
Full-time farmers, partners, active directors	150.9	111.5	-26%
Part-time farmers, partners, active directors	41.1	72.2	+76%
Salaried managers	5.3	6.9	+30%
Total other workers	320.1	191.0	-40%

Source: MAFF

This reduction in the agricultural labour force has been mirrored in all industrial countries. Farm workers leaving the industry have usually gone to better paid or otherwise more attractive jobs while mechanisation and other technological advances have meant that farmers have not needed to replace them.

Despite very high levels of support and protection under the CAP, farmers' incomes have generally been under pressure. Agricultural prices (including subsidies) have fallen substantially in real terms over the last 40 years, while costs have risen substantially, in part because the CAP itself has contributed to higher input costs. Only in the last few years has there been a marked recovery in farm income, largely because of the fall in the value of the pound sterling. This recovery would not have been feasible without the United Kingdom's successful resistance to the original MacSharry proposals which would have severely disadvantaged our own industry.

Productivity improvements and other developments have increased the optimum economic size of a farm. The number of agricultural holdings in England has fallen to 153,000, compared with 172,000 in 1976. Only 89,000 are considered to be full-time and they account for 98% of agricultural output. Generally speaking, farm enterprises are now more specialised and concentrated and there is less mixed farming.

Economic Significance

Excluding the crops we cannot grow in Britain, our farmers and growers produce nearly three quarters of the food and animal feed we consume. They contribute 1.2% to English GDP and form the basis of a dynamic food processing sector which accounts for nearly 500,000 jobs and is a significant exporter. They also underpin many successful ancillary industries, producing goods such as farm machinery and fertiliser and a wide range of services. So the farmer's contribution to employment must not be underrated.

Farming may have declined substantially in relative importance, particularly as a direct employer, but its efficiency and structure put it in a strong position to make the most of access to the wider European market - provided that the framework of CAP policies is right and that all those involved in the industry recognise the paramount importance of marketing and meeting the needs of the consumer.

Farm Diversification

Farmers increasingly look to diversify into activities other than agriculture in order to supplement their incomes. Much farm-based work (equivalent to almost 80,000 full-time jobs)[1] is now concerned with activities such as woodland management, running farm shops and equestrian businesses, and the provision of sporting facilities, nature trails, holiday cottages and various agricultural services. A study carried out in 1994 estimated that farm diversification generated £675 million of revenue annually[2].

Ministry of Agriculture, Fisheries and Food

Self-catering accommodation at Old Yates Farm, Abberley, Worcester. Guests have access to the farm and are able to participate in feeding calves

Adding Value on the Farm - Denhay Farms

Denhay Farms near Bridport in Dorset has for decades followed a traditional West Country farming cycle, in which milk from dairy cows is made into butter and cheese, with the whey fed to pigs whose muck is returned to enrich the grassland grazed by the cows. They make their Cheddar cheese in different sizes for different markets - ranging from traditional 25kg cylinders, through 20kg blocks to 2kg "Dorset Drums".

Seeing the need to add more value to and diversify the output of this farming enterprise, Denhay have developed the business by marketing their own air-dried ham. They are expecting to sell up to 2000 hams in 1995, either whole or thinly sliced and vacuum packed.

Overall, the business employs 60 people, and plans shortly to expand further into a new ham house, and more new bacon and pork products.

[1] *Source: Patterns, Performance and Prospects in Farm Diversification by the Agricultural Economics Unit, University of Exeter [ISSN 0306 8277]*
[2] *Non Farming Sources of Income: Their Incidence and Importance, The Produce Studies Group July 1994*

The Farm Diversification Grant Scheme introduced in 1988 helped to show the way forward. Today, we are continuing to promote diversification through publications and other forms of advice. MAFF has helped to set up Farm Attraction Groups to develop farms as tourist attractions. A sample survey in 1994 found that for member farms the enterprise made up, on average, 45% of the total business income of the farm[1]. This average figure covers a wide range, however, and on the majority of member farms the figure would be well below this level.

Alternative Crops

Diversification is taking place within agriculture as well as outside it. New crops and conventional crops grown for non-food uses have obvious attractions for farmers as an alternative to products which are in surplus. They may offer new rural employment opportunities in processing as well as agriculture. Developing the use of renewable raw materials for industrial feedstocks and energy could also contribute substantially to the sustainable development strategy. To put this in context, only a century ago farmers produced almost all of the energy and many of the raw materials they needed in order to work their farms, with feed for their horses, wood for fuel and some fibres. We would only be returning to historical practice if a significant area of land were devoted to raw material and energy crops.

Fields of flax outside Hampnett, Gloucestershire

Short rotation coppice

Coppice of willow or poplar can be grown in short rotations, using methods more commonly used on arable crops, and harvested once every 2-4 years to produce wood for fuel. Under the Non Fossil Fuel Obligation three projects, located in Yorkshire, Wiltshire and Suffolk, have won contracts to supply Regional Electricity Companies with electricity generated from short rotation coppice, using advanced conversion techniques. It is expected that over the next few years 5,000 to 7,000 hectares of short rotation coppice could be established to supply the three power stations. Additional areas may also be established to supply smaller heat or combined heat and power plants.

In July 1994, MAFF issued a consultation document on novel and industrial uses for agricultural crops, *Alternative Crops, New Markets*. It identified a number of areas with possibilities:

Coppice, harvested as whole sticks, being chipped by a tractor mounted chipper

- industrial oils and fatty acids;

- fuels including short rotation coppice and liquid biofuels;

- fibres;

- pharmaceuticals and other high value products;

- sugars, starches, polysaccharide gums and others.

---

[1] *National Farm Attractions Survey 1994 ADAS and John Brown and Company 1995*

For the future the key is to find new crops and new uses which have the potential to be commercially viable and environmentally beneficial overall. MAFF has increased spending on Research and Development for alternative crops to £1.3 million in 1995/96 and has set up an Alternative Crops Unit which is now working to encourage the development of new markets and business opportunities. It has commissioned new research projects on oils, fibres and biomass and, in July 1995, published its strategy for renewable raw materials for industry and energy.

Agriculture and the Environment

Landowners have a long-term interest in the productive capacity of their land and the sustainable use of natural resources. There is, however, increasing recognition that in recent years modern farming methods have had a substantial effect on the appearance of the countryside and the wildlife that it sustains. The draining of wetlands and the ploughing of botanically rich grasslands are among the undesirable effects of more intensive systems of farming.

The long tradition of unpaid stewardship by farmers and landowners is not always sufficient to ensure that they deliver all the environmental benefits that society now wants and expects. There are no market rewards to help support the maintenance of dry-stone walls or of flower-rich hay meadows. We therefore consider it right to provide appropriate incentives to farmers to deliver these environmental benefits. Our policies are described in more detail in Chapter Four.

The fact that expanding food production is no longer an overriding imperative provides a major opportunity to give a higher priority to environmental concerns, one to which we are responding actively both in terms of national policies and in the reforms which we have sought and continue to seek to the CAP.

The Common Agricultural Policy

Tractor and baler baling grass for silage in Devon

The CAP is the main determinant of public policy towards agriculture. It has provided security and other benefits for British and other European farmers and helped to provide our consumers with an unprecedented variety of high quality food. These successes must, however, be set against the excessive cost of the policy, much of which is attributable to the fact that it has stimulated food production well beyond what would have been accomplished by market forces on their own. Introduced in an era still influenced by memories of post-war food shortages, its very success had put the containment of overproduction at the top of the agenda by the 1980s.

Reforms in recent years have begun to tackle the problems of the CAP by reducing support prices for cereals, beef and butter. These reforms have also brought EC backing and finance to measures to encourage more environmentally friendly farming. Against this, the proliferation of supply controls, particularly quotas, has had very unwelcome effects, preventing rational economic development and creating barriers to young farmers and others wishing to enter the industry.

Enforcement of supply controls also inevitably requires a huge amount of bureaucracy and regulation. This means more paperwork for farmers and excessive government interference in their business decisions. The United Kingdom has consistently argued against supply controls and in favour of a market-oriented approach based on a further lowering of support prices and freer trade.

The case for further, fundamental reform of the CAP is, in the Government's view, unanswerable. The CAP:

- maintains a high-cost agriculture such that for many products European farmers cannot compete on world markets without subsidy;

- disadvantages consumers and the food industry by obliging them to pay artificially high prices for food and raw materials;

- is unduly expensive, with expenditure in the United Kingdom alone amounting to £2.7 billion in 1994/95;

- is wasteful - total transfer payments from EC consumers and taxpayers (including national budgetary expenditures) are estimated by OECD to have exceeded total EC farm income in 1993 by 50%;

- has in many instances provided incentives for production without due regard for environmental considerations.

We want to see an efficient, prosperous and outward-looking agricultural industry, able to operate in increasingly open world markets, providing high quality raw materials at competitive prices for the domestic food industry and paying due regard to the environment. The key to this lies with progressive reductions in production-related support and the eventual abolition of supply controls, within the continuing framework of a common EC agricultural policy avoiding competing national subsidies. Production patterns would then be determined much more by competition and relative efficiency. In order to help farmers to adjust, temporary compensation in the form of direct payments not linked to production may well be appropriate. Within such a policy there should continue to be scope for supplementary measures to help in situations such as the hill farming areas of Britain where there are particular reasons for maintaining extensive agriculture.

The goal of safeguarding and enhancing the rural environment should be at the heart of a reformed CAP, with policy mechanisms geared towards specific objectives. Progressive reductions in production-related support can be expected to yield large savings. Whilst it should not be assumed that all savings would automatically be available to farming or that action at the EC level would always be the best way to approach environmental objectives, a substantial level of public funding to secure environmental benefits would be justified.

Events likely to occur over the next few years will reinforce the need for far-reaching change. The commitments made by the European Community under the GATT Uruguay Round, the resumption of GATT negotiations in 1999 and the prospective enlargement of the European Union to include the countries of Central and Eastern Europe, are likely to make an unreformed CAP unsustainable beyond the turn of the century.

It is in all parties' interest for the EC to address these issues well in advance so that the necessary changes can be well prepared. **For the immediate future we will continue our efforts to secure more economically rational policies and to ensure that a higher proportion of EC expenditure on direct payments to farmers is directed towards the encouragement of environmentally beneficial and sustainable farming. We will also continue to oppose proposals for CAP reform which could disadvantage our farmers in the United Kingdom.**

Agricultural Education and Training

Industry representatives are concerned about the age profile of those in agriculture and horticulture businesses. Agriculture and horticulture are likely to remain capital intensive making access difficult for new entrants. As a result, many newcomers will enter the industry as farm managers rather than farm owners. In recognition of this, we will aim to ensure that educational courses equip college graduates to fulfil this rôle and that training continues to reflect the needs of entrants to the sector as well as those moving into new areas of business in the rural economy.

Industry Training Organisations represent most sectors of industry, and complement the local activities of TECs. ATB-Landbase fulfils this role for the agriculture and commercial horticulture sectors. While the cost of providing Industry Training Organisation services is normally met by industry, MAFF funds these activities and other services through a contract with ATB-Landbase worth £6.6 million for the two years to 31 March 1996. This work involves training, promotion, market research, development of vocational education and training standards, training materials, plus the provision of support for a network of training providers and instructors. **The present arrangements are being reviewed against the Government's policy objectives in order to inform decisions on future levels of support to the sector, as well as the most appropriate ways of providing it.**

Agricultural colleges too have a key rôle in helping to meet future industry training and education needs. The range of courses they offer has broadened significantly, reflecting the diversification of rural economic activity, as well as growing interests in leisure and business opportunities such as equestrianism. While the more traditional agricultural and horticultural subjects continue to be taught, new courses are emerging to complement them. The development of the key business skills, and the integration of environmental awareness into existing agriculture courses is becoming more important, mirroring the sector's future needs.

Tourism and Recreation

Visitors come to the countryside to enjoy the environment, to visit its historical and architectural attractions, and for recreation. Rural tourism is growing and makes an important contribution to the income of rural areas. Recreation is a major source of wealth for rural areas and activity holidays show particular potential. Day visitors to the English countryside are estimated to spend an average of just over £5 on each visit. With day visits totalling about 1.1 billion each year, this means an annual contribution to the economy of over £5.5 billion[1].

Pony trekking, Temple Newsam, West Yorkshire

[1] Source: *The 1994 UK Day Visits Survey. Summary available from the Countryside Commission*

Field Sports

Field sports include a wide range of activities such as hunting, shooting and angling. For many they are a traditional part of the rural way of life.

Ministry of Agriculture, Fisheries and Food

Field sports make a significant contribution to rural economic activity. Many individuals depend on these sports for their livelihoods and, as with other recreational uses of the countryside, there are spin-off benefits for local economies. The economic importance of field sports is particularly marked in some remoter parts of the countryside, such as the north Pennines. The national rural economy is estimated to benefit from a total annual expenditure on field sports of £2.7 billion. They provide a vital part of the income of many farm businesses.

Some field sports have a close and positive association with conservation. In many areas heather moorland is sustained by management for sporting purposes. We commend the excellent conservation work of the Game Conservancy Trust. We have provided support to the Game Conservancy Trust to enable them to provide advice to farmers and other land managers. A recent restructuring of the Trust's Advisory Service has enabled information on conservation issues to be made more widely available.

Angling is one of the most popular pastimes in the country, with around 2.9 million anglers in England and Wales. It has helped to provide a spur to the improvement of water quality in our rivers and streams. The improvement of water quality which comes about through the efforts of the National Rivers Authority has been of major benefit to fisheries and will be continued by the Environment Agency. We will continue to provide support for angling through the Sports Council, and plan to provide a substantial contribution to the cost of the Environment Agency's work on fisheries and water quality.

Some sports provoke strong views both in defence and in condemnation. It is not for the Government to take a view as to the intrinsic merits of any of these sports - that is a matter for individuals. But we do uphold the right of country people, and for that matter urban people too, to participate in legal forms of recreation. We believe that there is a need for greater tolerance and understanding where urban attitudes come into conflict with the traditional values of the countryside.

For this reason we introduced the new offence of aggravated trespass under the Criminal Justice and Public Order Act 1994. The offence is designed to protect those pursuing a lawful activity from intimidation and bullying. The police are now able to pre-empt trouble.

Rural tourism needs to develop in a way which draws on the character of the countryside and does not destroy the very asset on which its popularity depends. This means striking a balance between the needs of the visitor, the character of the local environment and the quality of life of the local community. These considerations were taken into account in new planning guidance on tourism issued in November 1992 Planning Policy Guidance note 21, *Tourism*. This emphasised the importance of sensitive design for both large and small scale tourist developments.

We have sought to develop and disseminate principles and good practice for sustainable rural tourism and established a Task Force on Tourism and the Environment in 1991. The Department for National Heritage, together with the Rural Development Commission, the Countryside Commission and the English Tourist Board, has commissioned a good practice guide for sustainable rural tourism, which will be published this autumn. We will encourage all those involved in managing tourism in the countryside to make full use of this guide.

Paul Webbs/Devon and Cornwall Rail P'ship

Fowey Valley Train Special at Golant

The Devon and Cornwall Rail Partnership

Six branch lines run through the rural areas of Devon and Cornwall, providing access to the countryside, small towns and resorts. The Devon and Cornwall Rail Partnership aims to ensure their survival by encouraging increased use for leisure and recreation purposes.

The Partnership draws upon the expertise of many local, public and private enterprises in undertaking a number of projects including the improvement of signs and station facilities, promoting the use of the line and identifying places of interest and activities such as walking and cycling in the surrounding areas. As a result of its work, the use of the network has increased, the environmental impact of visitors has been reduced and local communities have benefited from tourist spending in the area.

Rural tourism businesses are generally small and the industry is fragmented. It is therefore important for such businesses to work together in order to promote their area and to find new markets, for example for out-of-season weekend breaks. We will continue to emphasise the importance of close working between our agencies, the Tourist Boards, local authorities and other bodies, and of partnership with the private sector at local level to develop local strategies.

Green Flag International

The Rural Development Commission is supporting the establishment of a national database of rural tourism ventures. This will make available to tour operators and holiday makers around the world details of accommodation and leisure activities available in rural areas.

In February 1995, we published a joint programme of action with the Tourist Boards *Competing with the Best*[1] which should benefit smaller, independent businesses in particular. This is the first step in an evolving policy of more effective tourism sponsorship, and once this action programme has been delivered we will look to build on it in ways that will bring further benefits to rural areas and that will help the tourism industry to reach its full potential. The programme includes action to:

● improve the quality and profitability of serviced accommodation;

● make it easier to book domestic holidays, including strengthening accommodation booking systems;

● improve marketing.

[1] *Tourism : Competing with the Best, Department of National Heritage, 1995, J0087NJ*

Tourism : Competing with the Best

The programme includes action for:

- Improving the quality and profitability of serviced accommodation

Improvements in the Tourist Board's "Crown" classification and grading scheme, which covers hotels, guesthouses, farmhouses and bed and breakfast, should make it more widely used by consumers. A parallel initiative to compare the performance of 70 small hotels, including a substantial number in rural areas, will lead to the dissemination of guidance on how small operators can improve both quality and profitability.

- Making it easier to book domestic holidays, including strengthening accommodation booking systems

An industry working group is to be set up to look at the scope for developing domestic tourism packages, including countryside holidays, which will attract consumers because of the ease of booking.

- Improving marketing

The English Tourist Board is targeting domestic growth markets, such as short breaks and additional holidays. An £8 million campaign by the British Tourist Authority, London Tourist Board and the private sector will attract new first time visitors to England by promoting London as the gateway to all the other attractions which Britain has to offer. The British Tourist Board is also conducting research overseas to find out why people come, or do not come, to Britain. One study has already shown that the French are increasingly attracted to the British countryside.

Market Towns

Changes in agriculture, in the ways that agricultural materials are supplied and produce marketed, have removed the historic purpose of many smaller market towns. Wider changes too have contributed to the decline. These include centralisation of some professions and services in larger towns, changes in patterns of leisure activity and the development of out of town superstores.

Redruth, Cornwall

Yet small market towns provide important services and employment for their rural hinterland and their future well-being is essential for the vitality of surrounding villages. For some time, the Rural Development Commission has been involved in their regeneration in Rural Development Areas, mainly in partnership with the Civic Trust. It is now developing a wider initiative to help revitalise the centres of small market towns across the countryside and has sponsored two conferences to assess the problems and the action needed. It is now considering ways of taking forward some of the ideas generated. These include:

- encouraging a Market Town Forum or information network which will help market towns to share information and experience, and to develop and disseminate good practice;

- contributing to a guide for smaller towns on how to improve their future;

- funding a small number of demonstration projects, jointly with local authorities, businesses and others, to test innovative approaches.

We intend to strengthen our advice to local planning authorities on the need to take account of the impact of major new retail developments. In July 1995, we consulted on the revised draft of Planning Policy Guidance note 6, *Town Centres and Retail Developments*. We have proposed that local authorities should seek to ensure that supermarkets, wherever possible, are built in or on the edge of the town centre. We have commissioned research to examine the impact of out of town superstores on market towns. The results will help local authorities in their assessment of such proposals and Planning Inspectors in considering appeals.

Ministry of Agriculture, Fisheries and Food

Trawler being unloaded at Brixham, Devon

Fishing

Sea fishing takes place all around the coast but is particularly important in the South West, the North East and the North West, often based in small rural ports. In these areas, fishing and its associated industries are important for local employment.

Very few of the fish stocks which our fleet exploits are confined to our waters and therefore international co-operation is essential for their conservation. The Common Fisheries Policy provides the means for joint action with our neighbours. Currently our fishermen and other European fishermen are affected by the over exploitation of the fish stocks. We are funding a scheme to decommission vessels as a way of removing surplus capacity and thus achieving a more sustainable fisheries policy. Conservation is the key to the long term sustainability of fish stocks and therefore the viability of the industry.

We have set up a Review Group of independent people with experience of the fishing industry, economics, fisheries science and the environment. The Group is considering options for improving the Common Fisheries Policy. When we have the Group's report, we will consult about their ideas and then pursue in Brussels the most promising proposals.

Defence

Many major defence establishments, such as air bases, are located in rural areas. They frequently act as the main employer in a small community, and their closure can create substantial local problems.

We are committed to maximising the potential of redundant facilities for suitable employment and wealth creation. A range of regeneration programmes is available to help breathe new economic life into areas adversely affected by defence closures. We will ensure that decisions on disposal and re-use take account of policies for regeneration and land use for the local area. Development plans should take account of the potential of defence facilities. We are committed to making the best use of land which has already been developed, in order to reduce the need to build on greenfield sites. The Ministry of Defence (MOD) will:

● continue to improve its links with Government Offices, which have a key rôle to play in developing economic regeneration strategies and in working with local authorities on development plans; the potential of defence sites should be considered fully when these strategies and plans are drawn up. MOD and the Government Offices will develop and publish guidelines for joint working;

- consult with relevant local authorities who can help ensure that the needs of the local community are taken into account in the plans for the re-use of these sites;

- seek, with Government Offices, to work in partnership with more local planning authorities to draw up planning briefs for major sites;

- work with English Partnerships to help to bring sites into new uses;

- put together packages of land and property for sale which are attractive to developers and maximise economic potential;

- consider innovative ways of attracting new investment to redundant sites, such as joint ventures or use of the Private Finance Initiative.

In addition, we welcome bids from local partnerships to acquire sites as a way of maximising the benefits of regeneration for local people.

Telecommunications and Information Technology

Infrastructure

The widespread changes in the countryside which have resulted from the impact of technology on farming and fishing and from the reduction in defence commitments have been paralleled by a wider and perhaps more pervasive change. The microchip has made a real difference to all our lives but not least to the concept of remoteness. The computer, the fax, e-mail and the explosion in telecommunications may have their most radical effect in the countryside.

This has been made possible by our policy of privatisation and liberalisation in telecommunications which has encouraged greater competition and opened up this new world. Prices have fallen as services have improved. The majority of rural areas now have access to Integrated Services Digital Network (ISDN) services, which provide access to facilities such as on-line databases and transmission of graphics. All rural areas can gain access to digital exchanges.

Fibre optic cables which can carry large amounts of information are being installed around the country. Although rural areas are likely to benefit less quickly from this, the benefits will come through as the network grows.

Cambridge Cable Ltd

Cambridge Cable is installing broadband communications cable in Cambridge, Harlow, Southern East Anglia and Ipswich and Colchester. A substantial part of these areas is rural. Cambridge Cable is setting an example by ensuring that fibre optic cables are installed in rural as well as in urban areas, providing a high quality television and telephone network. Some 70,000 homes and businesses have been connected including some 20,000 in rural areas and market towns.

We will make radio spectrum available for low-cost, flexible links between telecommunications switching centres and customers. In particular, this will benefit businesses in remoter rural areas. We have sought comments on our proposals[1]. We will shortly announce the way in which spectrum will be made available and particular care will be taken to ensure that the benefits are available to rural areas.

All this opens up ways of improving access to training in rural areas and the Department for Education and Employment is supporting pilot projects with TECs and others to see how best to realise the potential.

Benefits and Take up

Telecommunications and information technology (IT) offer significant opportunities for rural enterprise. They enable some businesses to locate further from their customers than in the past and become more efficient and competitive. We want to see more rural businesses take up the opportunities offered by this technology. But still too few are aware of the potential and we are determined to spread the word more effectively:

- our strategic guidance to the TECs recommends that their local strategies should promote the use of IT and improve telecommunications infrastructures;

- Business Links will use new technology, including e-mail and videoconferencing, to bring local firms into contact with prospective clients and suppliers across the country.

Working Practices

Using a modem, teleworkers maintain links with remote computer networks and communicate with colleagues and clients through e-mail. By raising awareness of the potential of IT we will help people in rural communities to realise the benefits of teleworking. To this end the then Employment Department published "A Manager's Guide to Teleworking" in May 1995, to give advice to managers considering the introduction of teleworking.

Wiltshire TEC

Wiltshire TEC has funded a free two day course for women wanting to work from home, either in a business or as a self-employed teleworker. The course covered issues such as the effective use of time and space and ways of negotiating new patterns of behaviour and routine with family and friends.

The United Kingdom has over 120 telecottages, mostly small business centres, which provide access to computers and IT. In rural areas, telecottages can help to overcome the isolation which some teleworkers feel. They can also provide training for local people who wish to learn new computer skills or market their existing skills. The Rural Development Commission (RDC) and the TECs have assisted with the setting up of a number of telecottages in rural areas and the RDC has grant aided the development of the Telecottage Association, which acts as a source of support and advice for telecottages.

[1] *"Radio Fixed Access - Increasing the Choice, A Consultative Document", Department of Trade and Industry May 1995*

The RDC has also commissioned research to assess the viability and potential of telecottages in rural England, and to examine the likely developments in teleworking over the next decade and how these developments may affect rural areas. Further research will look at the implications for rural areas of changes in telecommunications infrastructure in the foreseeable future.

Acorn Televillages

Rapid developments in telecommunications are creating new opportunities including for teleworkers. Perton Farm telehamlet, for example, near Wolverhampton, uses new technology and redundant farm buildings to allow a mix of people to live and work together within one community, reducing the need to travel to work. The buildings are sensitively converted using local materials and craftsmen, have high energy efficiency standards and have been commended for the quality of their design.

Perton Farm telehamlet, completed by Acorn in 1991, was the prototype for the televillage concept

Likely Developments

It seems certain that more people will have computers at home both for work and for leisure purposes. Distance learning, home shopping and direct banking have obvious benefits for rural areas. The United Kingdom is a world leader in the application of modern technology to training and we intend to encourage the application of this knowledge, particularly in rural areas. We see rural areas especially as targets for advice and information in helping employers and individuals to make use of technology in training. Our Technology Foresight programme has identified trends which will be relevant to the use of information technology in rural areas including the development of networks from local to international levels. Chapter Three describes some ways in which information technology is being used to deliver public services, including, in some areas, medical information and diagnosis.

Technology Foresight

This programme is a major initiative to identify promising new technologies for the future, the market opportunities to exploit them and their effects on the quality of life in the United Kingdom. The recommendations of its 15 panel reports cover the complete spectrum of United Kingdom industry and many are relevant to rural communities. For example, the Agriculture, Natural Resources and Environment panel recommended investment in research on a range of topics including predictive modelling to help farmers use agrochemicals more efficiently, and plant and animal biotechnology for more efficient production of crops and livestock.

3. LIVING IN THE COUNTRYSIDE

INTRODUCTION

To many, perhaps a majority of those who live in towns and cities, the idea of countryside living is synonymous with a better quality of life. The attractions are such that the rural population has been growing rapidly. In the 1980s it expanded by more than 7%, over twice the national average. Population in the remoter rural areas grew faster than in the areas around the towns, indicating that the force at work is far more than the product of urban overspill and that a home in the countryside has become a popular aspiration.

This is perhaps not surprising. Whereas in France the symbol of success is to live in a smart flat in the best *arrondissement* in Paris, in England it has been to live in a house in the country. What has happened more recently is that the long-standing preference of the rich has been popularised so that it is an achievable aspiration of the much more modestly placed.

Yet the attractiveness of the countryside as a place to live can easily disguise the fact that rural society faces its full share of problems. Rates of pay, especially in traditional rural occupations such as agriculture and tourism, are generally below those in urban areas, a disadvantage often compounded by the seasonality of the work. Although unemployment is below the national average, there are nonetheless problems associated with underemployment and low income, often cheek-by-jowl with relative affluence. These problems may be less visible and more dispersed than in the town but rural deprivation brings its own disadvantages, particularly in terms of access to services.

Rural Housing

One of the most pressing concerns of those on low incomes is the limited availability of housing which they can afford to rent or to buy. Rising demand for homes in the countryside, not least from people with well-paid employment in urban areas, has raised prices in large areas of the country, particularly within commuting distance of the towns. This effect is likely to persist because the supply of housing in rural areas is limited - the planning system necessarily exists to ensure that development takes place in a manner which is acceptable and does not destroy the unique character of the countryside.

We believe that people, particularly young people, who have grown up in the countryside should have a reasonable prospect of finding affordable housing rather than being forced to move into the towns. It is central to the principle of sustainable development that jobs and housing should, where possible, be located so as to avoid the need for long journeys to work. There is also much to be said for maintaining close-knit and balanced communities where, for example, the elderly can find support from the young and vice versa.

Rural Services and Transport

The limited availability of services in rural areas is a matter which concerns all who live in the countryside. Most people's ideal village would have at least its own church, shop, post office, primary school, village hall, doctor, pub and regular public transport. The Rural Development Commission's 1994 Survey of Rural Services shows a picture which falls a long way short of this ideal.

Results of Rural Development Commission Survey of Rural Services in 1994

- 59% of parishes have a permanent shop and 57% a post office;

- 48% of parishes have a state school of some sort;

- 17% of parishes have a permanently based GP;

- 41% of parishes have a church or chapel with a resident minister;

- 71% of parishes have a village hall or community centre;

- 87% of parishes have a bus service, with 29% reporting a daily service and 36% reporting a service six days a week;

- 2% of parishes have a permanently staffed police station;

- 70% of parishes have a pub.

The fact is that there has been a steady decline in the services permanently based in villages over recent decades. The principal causes are:

- the trend towards centralisation in order to achieve economies of scale and to provide more advanced facilities;

- the acceleration of this trend arising from the development of more specialised, sophisticated and expensive technologies, for example in medicine and policing;

- the growth of modern communications and transport, in particular the inexorable growth in the use of the private motor car.

It is the growth of private car ownership which has been the most pervasive force for change in the last 50 years. Increasing car ownership has been both cause and effect of the decline in services. Increased personal mobility has given many the means to travel further afield to shops, banks or leisure facilities. This has helped undermine the viability not only of local services but also of rural public transport, making private transport a virtual necessity.

People in rural areas are clearly more dependent on the car than their counterparts in town. This is reflected in the higher proportion of rural households with access to a car - an average of 77% across rural areas as against 68% nationally. For many in the countryside, the car is no longer a luxury which can be given up when times are hard. For those without a car, the decline in public transport which has mirrored the growth in car journeys is a serious handicap. This group includes many pensioners, young, unemployed, sick or disabled people and - particularly during the daytime - mothers with young children.

Objectives

Notwithstanding these developments, we do not accept that the further erosion of rural services and the institutions of village life is inevitable. Thriving communities with a healthy future are an important part of our strategy for sustainable development. Communities will not thrive unless people's basic needs - for housing, shopping, transport and other services - are met. Our policies will therefore seek to:

- foster living rural communities with a mixture of age groups and economic activities;

- reverse the general decline in rural services so that people have reasonable access to the services they need, regardless of where they live;

- improve the performance of public services, making them more responsive to the needs of rural people;

- help communities to strengthen their public and voluntary institutions so that they can meet their own needs;

- promote innovative and cost-effective ways of meeting the everyday needs of rural communities.

West Sussex County Council

Village Information Point in a shop in West Sussex. Through the terminals, local residents have easy access to a range of valuable information about various aspects of public services in the county. In addition, people can look up information about clubs and societies, details of Adult Education courses, Social Security benefits and bus timetables. The presence of the terminal enhances the shop's focal role as a centre for the community.

Innovative Approaches

Much can be done to revitalise our rural communities, building on their traditional strengths of communal action, enterprise and voluntary activity. More flexible approaches are needed. New technology offers exciting possibilities, enabling information, financial and even medical services to be accessed remotely although mobile facilities too can play a part. There is scope for cost-saving in the sharing and multiple use of facilities such as school buildings. There are many examples of innovation and creativity in the delivery of services in the countryside. We will encourage service providers to learn from each other's experience by supporting the dissemination of best practice.

Many of the answers must lie in the hands of local people seeking local solutions to local problems, whether it is the entrepreneur who can provide a service tailored to actual needs, or a local group of volunteers. It is vital that there should be a continuing nationwide exchange of information on local successes and best practice. The many organisations and interest groups active in the countryside have a rôle to play here.

Community Radio

Community radio can cater directly for the tastes and interests of individual listeners. Complementing the services provided by BBC local radio and Independent Local Radio stations, it can play a particularly useful role in scattered communities, where it can cover issues and provide useful information which might be too local for other broadcasters.

Community radio now has the opportunity to expand. The Broadcasting Act 1990 made it easier to launch community stations and extended the opportunity for would-be operators to test the market and gain experience through broadcasting for short periods. The Radio Authority has earmarked an FM frequency range (107-108 MHz) for small local services and is ready to consider applications for licences. As a result, we anticipate a major increase in the number of stations operating.

Public Services

Rural people, including the least well off and those without their own transport, should have access to good publicly funded services, whether the responsibility of central or local government. Where the population is dispersed, service providers will not always be as close to all their customers as they are in cities. Rural people know and understand this. However, they are entitled to reasonable provision and to high quality services provided efficiently.

The **Citizen's Charter** programme aims to set high standards of public service. The publication of national charters such as the Parents' and Patients' Charters is already transforming the way in which service providers approach their task. The

One of Northumbria Ambulance Service NHS Trust's Land Rover Discovery ambulances. The Trust was the first ambulance service to be awarded a Charter Mark

Charter Mark scheme rewards excellence in service delivery. Organisations serving rural areas, such as Lincolnshire Police and Barrow Advice Centre, are among the Charter Mark winners.

The Citizen's Charter

Service providers should check how well they are meeting the needs of their rural customers against the six Charter principles which should underpin all public services:

- **Standards:** Providers may need to adopt innovative means of ensuring that standards are met in rural areas, as overall standards may hide local differences in the quality of provision.
- **Information and Openness:** Provision of information about services may be more difficult in rural areas. Service providers should examine whether they have done as much as they can to make information as readily available and as easy to obtain as possible.
- **Choice and Consultation:** Service providers should, wherever practicable, provide choice. Increased choice may reduce the problems of access which some people in rural areas face. Service providers also need to understand the particular needs and views of rural inhabitants and to take these into account.
- **Courtesy and Helpfulness:** Services should be run with users in mind. Opening times in rural areas may need to take account of local circumstances such as public transport timetables and market days.
- **Putting Things Right:** Procedures for lodging complaints, suggestions and compliments should be publicised in such a way that all users are aware of them.
- **Value for money:** Costs of delivery may be higher in rural areas than in the town. Providers can examine innovative ways of reducing costs, through for example the sharing of facilities such as village halls, schools and libraries.

Charter Mark Winners

Lincolnshire Police

Lincolnshire Police have launched a Community Volunteers Programme. Sixty local volunteers, drawn from a wide range of backgrounds, regularly staff rural police stations, primarily in the evenings and at weekends. Police officers are thus able to devote more time to patrolling and do not have to be called back long distances to deal with non-urgent matters. A mobile police station, which contains a crime prevention display, tours villages and communities throughout the county.

Barrow Advice Centre

This Centre provides comprehensive family healthcare advice in Barrow and the surrounding area. It seeks to ensure that the public are informed of its services in a number of ways. These include taking a mobile display to agricultural shows and exhibitions throughout south Cumbria.

We now wish further to encourage those who provide services in rural areas to take account of the particular needs of their customers. We will do so by launching a Rural Charter Initiative within the framework of the Citizen's Charter.

Under the Rural Charter Initiative we shall:

● publish a rural services Charter Checklist, which will help service providers to see whether they are meeting the needs of their rural customers. The Checklist is being prepared in consultation with service providers and community organisations: three workshops were held during the summer of 1995 , at which views were sought on what the Checklist should contain;

● hold a rural services seminar, which will take place shortly as part of the Charter Quality seminar series, providing an opportunity for a wide-ranging discussion of the issues relating to rural service delivery.

Customers too have their part to play. They need to recognise the particular difficulties of providing services in rural areas and draw upon the traditions of independence, partnership and voluntary action to help overcome them.

Living Communities

Ultimately, the quality of life in the countryside depends crucially on the people who live and work there. The influx of former town dwellers into rural areas is said by some to have undermined the traditional closeness of village life and to have encouraged resistance to local economic development. It is not for Government to determine who should live where, but we do want to see living rural communities with a balance of age groups and a range of local jobs and services. Our policies on matters such as housing, transport, schools and village shops will continue to be guided by that vision.

HOUSING

The White Paper on Housing, *Our Future Homes: Opportunity, Choice, Responsibility*, published in June 1995, sets out our housing policies for England and Wales. It confirms our commitment to enable everyone to have a choice of decent housing. In rural as in urban areas, we are working to ensure decent housing through sustainable growth in home ownership, increased choice in renting, a healthy private rented sector and the provision of social housing for those in need.

Rural Housing: Key Facts

- 75% of rural housing is owner-occupied compared to 64% of urban housing.

- The private rented sector, including tied housing, is more significant in rural than in urban areas.

- There is less social housing in rural than in urban areas: around 12% of housing compared to 25% in urban areas.

England faces increasing demand for housing because of the rising numbers of single person households and elderly people living apart from their families. In addition, there are special factors to be taken into account in rural areas. These include demand from incomers with town-based jobs or those retiring to the country, the rising rural population and the restricted availability of sites for new housing. The strength of these pressures will vary but in some rural areas they can make it difficult for people who work locally to find affordable housing.

Most new homes are built by private enterprise for owner occupation. We aim to create the conditions for private investment including a planning system which enables enough homes to be built or converted. In support of our belief that the countryside should contain diverse communities where people live, work and meet, our housing policy for rural areas aims to ensure that:

- local people are not priced out of the market;

- the right size and type of homes are built for those wishing to rent, for first-time buyers and those with low incomes.

Earls Manor Court sheltered housing, Winterbourne (Architect: Sidell Green Partnerships)

Affordable housing in Stiffkey, Norfolk. Built with a flint and brick design, the new homes fit with the local character

Stonesfield Community Trust

Energy-efficient homes built by Stonesfield Community Trust, Oxfordshire, for letting at affordable rents to local young couples and single people of all ages (Architect: CB Wilcher)

Affordable Housing

Around 6% of the new development programmes for housing under the Housing Corporation's Rural Housing Programme is targeted at rural settlements with a population of 3,000 or less. The majority of the programme is directed at villages of less than 1,000 population. Rural communities are given priority in this way because small schemes can require more effort to get off the ground and do not usually benefit from economies of scale.

The Programme was introduced in 1989/90, since when it has provided some 10,800 homes. We wish to build on this success and will do so as resources permit. We will also look at ways to ensure that the resources are spent where they are most needed.

The Rural White Paper consultation revealed concerns about the costs of developing small schemes in villages. We have therefore agreed that the Housing Corporation should introduce, from 1996-97, a rural village "enhancement factor" to its grants to housing associations and other providers. This will increase the amount of Government subsidy to individual schemes in settlements of up to 3,000 people by up to a quarter. It will provide new incentives for local authorities and housing associations to give priority to village housing.

The Housing White Paper announced proposals to give a wider range of landlords the opportunity to provide homes for social renting. This would be done by allowing private sector bodies other than housing associations to bid for Housing Association Grant. Those who could bid would include private landlords or landowners and charitable bodies interested in social housing in rural areas.

Government's Housing Strategy for Rural Areas

1. Encourage a wide range of housing options to maintain balanced, living communities, serving all aspects of housing need.

2. Take particular measures to secure the provision of affordable housing in the countryside, including:

   • targeting resources for new affordable housing in the smallest communities through the Housing Corporation's Rural Housing Programme;

   • enabling local planning authorities to give permission for affordable housing outside areas allocated for development in the development plan (the "rural exceptions" policy: see below).

3. Ensure that the planning system provides an adequate supply of land for housing to meet local needs in terms of a range of sizes and affordability.

4. Enable people who work in the countryside to live locally, so minimising the need to travel.

5. Make best use of the existing housing stock, including conversions to meet the growing need for homes for small households.

6. Ensure that new housing is of appropriate design and scale.

7. In the longer term, relieve pressure on the countryside by making cities more attractive places in which to live.

Planning

Planning Policy Guidance note 13, *Transport* emphasises the need for local planning authorities to consider the interrelationship between housing and economic development, with a view to enabling people to live close to where they work and to reduce the need to travel. Planning Policy Guidance note 7 *The Countryside and the Rural Economy* complements this policy by encouraging the provision of suitable new housing in villages in order to support the local rural economy and village vitality and protect the open countryside.

Lealholm, North Yorkshire

In many rural areas there are particular difficulties in securing an adequate supply of land for affordable housing. In 1989 we introduced the "exceptions" policy which allows local planning authorities to give permission for small scale schemes, purely for affordable housing, within or adjoining villages, where the land is not designated for housing in the development plan. This helps to reduce the price of the land. It must however be demonstrated that there is a need for affordable housing locally to justify the "exception". In order to encourage further this type of arrangement, homes in rural areas will be exempt from the new Purchase Grant Scheme (see below).

Planning policy guidance stipulates that isolated new houses in the open countryside require special justification - for example where they are essential to enable farmworkers to live at or near their place of work. This agricultural concession continues to be needed by genuine farmers and their employees, but it should not be abused. We will publish research into its operation and consult on ways of strengthening it. We are also determined that imaginative schemes for isolated dwellings should not always be dismissed. There must be scope for the truly original and high quality building which enhances its surroundings.

Extending Home Ownership

Home ownership brings benefits for the individual and for society and we have given the "right to buy" to over 5 million tenants of councils, New Towns and housing associations. In the countryside it is necessary to make the best use of a more limited supply of affordable housing in the interests of those on low income. Certain restrictions can be placed on the right to buy in some areas to ensure that the housing remains available for local people.

In National Parks, Areas of Outstanding Natural Beauty (AONBs) or other areas designated by the Secretary of State for the Environment as rural, the onward sale of property purchased under the right to buy can be limited to people who have been living or working in the region for at least three years[1].

1 *"Region" is defined as including the National Park, AONB or rural area defined by the Secretary of State and the county in which the house is situated.*

In conjunction with the Housing White Paper we published a consultation paper on a new Purchase Grant Scheme to enable housing association tenants to buy their homes. The consultation document proposed special arrangements to safeguard the supply of affordable housing in rural areas.

In the light of responses to that document, the difficulties there can be in replacing properties in rural areas and the need to encourage the provision of affordable housing through planning exceptions, we have decided that all housing in communities of less than 3,000, including those in National Parks and AONBs, should be excluded from the proposed Purchase Grant Scheme.

Second Homes

A number of respondents to the Rural White Paper consultation raised concerns about the impact of second homes and holiday homes on local housing markets. Although second homes can be significant in particular areas - 60% of all second homes are located in the South West - they account for only about 2.5% of rural dwellings.

We do not consider that the incidence of second homes creates problems which justify changing national policies. Second homes and holiday homes can add to the vitality of rural areas by bringing in new people and new resources.

Private Rented Sector

Many landowners are reluctant to take on the hard work of managing tenants and property directly. We are looking for new ways of encouraging them to release more of their housing stock for rent. We recently introduced a new programme to encourage housing associations to act as managing agents for property they do not own and will consider how to encourage this trend in rural areas, with a particular focus on bringing empty property back into use.

In order to encourage more people to rent out vacant property, the Housing White Paper announced our commitment to introduce legislation aimed at simplifying letting arrangements and allowing small landlords to act more quickly when a tenant does not pay the rent. We will also encourage greater investment in private sector rented housing by providing tax concessions for new housing investment trusts.

We welcome the research project on private renting in rural areas being undertaken by Professor Peter Kemp at the University of York and funded by the Joseph Rowntree Foundation. This is looking at the contribution of the private rented sector in rural areas of England and Wales, including how country landowners might be encouraged to retain, modernise and expand their rented property holdings. The Country Landowners Association is actively involved in the project which is also supported by an advisory group representing a range of rural interests, including the Rural Development Commission. The project is expected to report in the summer of 1996. We will review our policies to encourage the private rented sector in rural areas in the light of this research.

Local Housing Strategies

Local authorities are required to draw up housing strategies which determine their priorities and guide the distribution of resources from the Housing Corporation. A high priority for rural housing in an authority's strategy is important if the Housing Corporation is to be able to respond effectively. Government guidance to local authorities on housing strategies will encourage authorities with a significant rural population to develop specific rural housing policies as a component of their housing strategies.

Rural housing policies should take account of the state of repair of property. Local authority housing in rural areas is generally in a worse condition than similar property in urban areas. Housing associations may be better placed to carry out repairs and transferring property to them may therefore help bring about improvement.

One of our important objectives is to increase the energy efficiency of the rural housing stock. The situation in rural areas is less satisfactory than in urban areas. 32% of rural council housing has an energy efficiency standard assessment procedure (SAP) rating of less than 20 compared with 16% of urban council housing and 15% of the stock as a whole. We expect local authorities to promote energy efficiency across all types of housing, and to integrate the concept into their housing strategies and programmes. We will also continue to review the effectiveness of our energy efficiency campaigns to establish whether there are any particular factors affecting awareness in rural areas.

Neighbourhood Energy Action

Neighbourhood Energy Action (NEA) has developed effective partnerships with energy companies to promote energy efficiency in rural communities. This has resulted in improved energy efficiency in housing, particularly that occupied by low income, disabled and elderly people, and in community buildings such as village halls. A good example is NEA's work with rural communities in Staffordshire and the Forest of Dean, which is supported by Midlands Electricity.

Council tenant in Longnor receiving advice as part of the Staffordshire scheme managed by Heatwise Staffordshire and Staffordshire Moorlands District Council and supported by Midlands Electricity

Rural housing policies can encourage the linking of rural tenancies with people who want to live in a particular settlement for family or employment reasons. We welcome moves by some local authorities and housing associations to develop common housing registers. Increasingly, local authorities and housing associations are cooperating to enable people to live closer to where they have local connections.

Rural Housing Enablers

We recognise that additional resources alone are not enough to secure more housing in rural areas. Determination and commitment from local individuals is also necessary, whether in carrying out local housing needs surveys or in negotiating with local landowners.

We are therefore pleased to support the Rural Development Commission's new scheme to fund Rural Housing Enablers. These will be independent people who will work closely with local authorities, housing associations, local communities, landowners, developers and other partners to facilitate and speed up co-ordination of development packages and to secure planning permission.

West Lindsay Rural Housing Enabler

The Rural Housing Enabler (RHE) post was created in 1991 as part of a pilot project run by Action with Communities in Rural England, funded by the Joseph Rowntree Foundation and the Rural Development Commission, with the objective of increasing the supply of affordable rural housing. The post has continued after the pilot phase with 50% of the funding now provided by the district council, and the remainder drawn from three housing associations, the House Builders Federation and charitable sources. The variety of funders helps to maintain the RHE's independence. The RHE is supported by a local advisory group which includes the main funders, the Lincolnshire Rural Community Council and local parish councils. Working as a catalyst and broker the RHE helps parish councils to identify their housing needs for example through local needs surveys. The RHE also assists local communities and the local planning department to find suitable sites and helps to facilitate the development process, ensuring the full involvement of the local community.

To date the work of the RHE has resulted in 20 units being built for rent in five villages, with a further 22 units in two other villages due to begin construction in the current year. Twenty-three villages have undertaken detailed surveys of their housing needs and 50 villages have taken advantage of the advisory service offered by the RHE. In addition the RHE has organised two local conferences and attended a large number of public meetings to raise awareness of rural housing issues and how they can be tackled.

Other agencies can also play a role in helping to facilitate rural housing. For example, large housing associations with large asset bases can work in partnership with smaller housing associations which offer the benefits of local trust and knowledge.

Making the Best Use of Existing Housing

Empty homes are a wasted resource. They are not just a feature of urban areas. Most empty property is privately owned and bringing it into use for private letting can help meet needs for affordable housing as well as reducing the need for new development. Measures to bring empty property back into use will continue to be an important element of local authority housing strategies. Local authorities are encouraged to:

- keep their stock of empty homes to a minimum and reduce underoccupation in their areas;

- develop measures, in partnership with housing associations, to improve the availability of suitable alternative accommodation for underoccupying tenants;

- use Rural Housing Enablers to help reduce underoccupation by achieving a better match between people's needs and the housing stock;

- use planning policies to encourage the conversion of existing houses into smaller units or flats where these might meet local needs more effectively.

We are also providing support to the Empty Homes Agency to help local authorities to develop empty property strategies in partnership with owners, landlords and other housing providers, including housing associations.

Lincolnshire Rural Housing Association

Sometimes housing needs arise in villages at relatively short notice. With the Housing Corporation's encouragement, Lincolnshire Rural Housing Association has pursued a policy over the past two years of purchasing existing satisfactory properties to meet these needs. This allows them to provide homes without the lengthy wait normally associated with completely new development. Needs are promptly met without the association having to bear any development risk.

The Government itself is a significant owner of empty housing. The Ministry of Defence (MOD) owns over 13,000 empty homes in Great Britain, many of which are in rural areas. Some 19% of the housing owned by MOD is standing empty. This vacancy rate is far too high and we are committed to reducing it significantly.

In 1995, we established the Defence Housing Executive (DHE) to ensure better management of MOD's housing. The new organisation is responsible for managing the estate and identifying surplus property for disposal. MOD aims to dispose of 4,000 surplus properties by the summer of 1996. Many more properties will be identified for disposal and, to speed up the selling process, surplus properties will be auctioned if no sale is in progress after six months. Monitoring procedures will be improved to ensure that this target is met. DHE will also make better use of properties which are temporarily vacant, by leasing these to local people wherever possible.

Housing for Young People

Young people are vital to the future of rural communities. While some will want to move away to pursue careers or courses of study, or simply to enjoy city life, it is crucial that they should not be forced to leave just because they have nowhere suitable and reasonably priced to live. Young people need a variety of housing ranging from hostels to their own homes.

The majority of the houses provided by the Housing Corporation's Rural Programme have been for families. However, the Housing Corporation's recently published rural policy guide emphasises the need, in designing housing schemes, to consider housing for young people, and the overall balance of the community. It encourages bodies carrying out surveys of local housing needs to consider the requirements of single people in the area. We have also drawn attention to the particular difficulties faced by young single people in our guidance to local authorities on drawing up housing strategies.

Lodgings could make a significant contribution to meeting housing need for young people. Very few households take in lodgers even when they have the space to do so. Research shows that rural households are more likely to have spare space than urban households. We intend to promote widely the benefits of having lodgers, including the opportunity under the Rent a Room Scheme to receive £3,250 rent tax free in any year without having to fill in a tax form.

Quality and Design

In order to preserve the beauty of the countryside, new housing developments in rural areas need to be designed and sited with particular care and sensitivity. They should respect the principles of good design, such as responsiveness to local distinctiveness. Chapter Four describes our Quality Initiative and the steps we are taking to improve the quality of the building in the countryside.

TRANSPORT

The Importance of Private Transport

In the countryside, private transport is now the key to maintaining the rural quality of life, a point which was made repeatedly in the responses to the consultation exercise on this White Paper.

For the great majority, rural transport is synonymous with use of a motor car. The National Travel Survey shows that in 1991-93 over two thirds of journeys in rural areas were by car or van compared with the national average of about half. Public transport alternatives are often limited and may not offer sufficient flexibility. There are many places where public transport could never be a viable option, nor would it be the best option environmentally. For these reasons, people in rural areas may have no choice but to spend a higher proportion of their incomes on cars than people in cities. There are proportionally more car-owning households in rural areas and also more households owning two or more cars. However, the ownership of two cars may not be a luxury in rural areas, especially where at least one of the cars is used for commuting to work.

Any sensible transport policy for rural areas must start from these realities and recognise that an adequate road network is as important to the inhabitants of an area as it is to its businesses and farms.

The remainder of this section sets out our policies towards the provision of public and community transport in rural areas. Policies on the environmental impact of private and other forms of transport are described in Chapter Four.

Buses

For the foreseeable future timetabled buses will continue to be the most widely used form of public transport in the countryside. Almost all bus services are provided commercially by private operators but we have given county councils the power to subsidise additional services where they consider this to be socially desirable. As a result, in the English shire counties, 18% of all bus mileage in 1993/94 was subsidised at a cost of some £90 million.

Information about timetabling of routes and the connections between different forms of transport such as buses and trains is especially important in rural areas. The wait for the next bus or train is often a long one. We therefore welcome the increasing number of telephone information services provided by local authorities and the bus industry. The provision of better travel information is identified in our "Technology Foresight" programme as an area where new technology can make a real difference. This could be of particular benefit in rural areas.

Cumbria Journey Planner

The Cumbria Journey Planner was run as a pilot project in the summer of 1994. Based on an existing database, details of all bus and train services in the county and on major routes to other cities were placed on a computer disk which can be bought by individuals, as well as tourist centres, libraries and hotels. Cumbria County Council hope to maintain the project for the next five years, providing winter and summer editions as well as regular updates to subscribers.

Innovative Responses

Conventional public transport is not always the right answer to the transport needs of rural areas and may involve unduly expensive subsidy. Moreover, buses which carry few people are not always the best environmental option. Solutions to rural transport needs must increasingly involve more flexible and innovative approaches, targeted on local circumstances and drawing on the resourcefulness of the community.

Volunteers can make a vital contribution to life in rural areas, for example by running car sharing schemes and driving mini buses. The Government's "Make a Difference" volunteering initiative will help volunteers to do even more in the future.

Villager Community Bus Service

Established in 1982, Villager Community Bus Services Ltd serves 300 square miles of the north Cotswolds and west Oxfordshire. The company provides an extensive coverage to some 60 villages, carrying over 17,000 passengers a year. They offer between one journey a fortnight on some routes and 28 journeys a week on others, and they can maintain services even when a bus is out of action. The drivers come from a pool of 25 volunteers. Only six of its seventeen routes receive operating subsidies from county councils, yet Villager Community Bus is able to meet its cost from fares, despite the highest price being 80 pence for a twenty mile journey. Villager carries children so that small village schools can have joint special activities at minimal expense.

Villager Community Bus Services Ltd

Parish councils are well placed to develop flexible transport solutions to meet community needs. We wish to enable parish councils to take a more active role in:

- conducting surveys to establish the transport needs of the community;

- providing support for community minibuses;

- contracting with local taxi companies to provide transport for the most needy members of the community;

- organising car sharing schemes;

- providing information on local transport services.

Legislation would be necessary to enable parish councils to take on these additional functions if they wish. The powers provided would not go beyond those available to district and county councils under the 1985 Transport Act. We are inviting comments on these broad proposals by March 1996[1] and will hold discussions with the Local Authority Associations.

The Government provides financial support for community transport in the countryside through the Rural Development Commission's Rural Transport Development Fund (RTDF). At present, the fund helps to provide local timetabled services available to the general public. These may not always provide the best means of meeting the needs of the local community, particularly those of children, the elderly and the disabled. We will therefore make the RTDF more flexible and remove some of the present restrictions. As this will stimulate greater demand for RTDF funding, we will give priority to the RTDF in future allocations of resources.

A lot of transport is provided in the countryside to meet particular needs. For example, there are minibuses to take people to day care centres and school buses to take children to school. These services could provide transport to a wider range of people. By using existing resources more flexibly, a better service can sometimes be provided at little extra cost. Some local authorities have shown what can be achieved by coordinating and integrating their various transport services.

In consultation with local authorities and the Rural Development Commission, we will produce a best practice guide to encourage wider adoption of this approach. The Rural Transport Development Fund is also available to support transport coordinators in making better use of existing transport

East Sussex County Rider

Access to services is not just about increasing people's mobility, but also trying to integrate public transport provision with the planning of service provision. In East Sussex, the public transport team contribute to the development of education and community care services. Discussions also involve parish councils, other professions and voluntary organisations, including community transport operators. This facilitates a greater understanding of the travel needs of people in rural areas, and how they might be met.

---

[1] *Comments should be sent to Steven Watts, Rm N7/16, Department of the Environment, 2 Marsham Street, London, SW1P 3EB.*

Because these operations are part-funded by other agencies, there is scope for low-cost innovation, for example the development of more frequent village shopping services and rural dial-a-ride. Many of these innovative services can be concentrated in the deep rural areas, leaving conventional bus services to concentrate on providing reasonably frequent inter-urban routes.

Post buses provide another excellent example of a creative response, building on an existing resource. Each year 150,000 people in the United Kingdom use post buses. Over the last four years, the number of routes has increased from 170 to 228, partly as a result of the £151,000 which the Rural Development Commission has provided to help establish new routes. The Post Office hopes to open 20 new routes each year for the next 3 years. It welcomes approaches from local authorities, parish councils and others to discuss the potential for post buses in areas where there is limited public transport.

Post bus in Cumbria

Railways

Privatisation of British Rail will protect rural rail services. Many rural rail services, like some bus services, will never be economic. That is why subsidy will continue to be available for socially necessary services. In addition - under the franchising arrangements - users of rural rail services will for the first time have the benefit of contractually binding guarantees for levels of service. The guarantees will safeguard services on every line and to every station in the country. Moreover, the Government's commitment to regulating rail fares will mean that key rail fares[1] will increase by no more than inflation for the next three years and will decrease in real terms for four years thereafter.

Privatisation and franchising offer new opportunities to enhance the use of lines and stations. Private sector operators will have incentives to provide innovative services to encourage the use of rural lines and flexibility to increase service provision where they judge it to be in their interests to do so. There will also be opportunities for partnerships between the private sector and local government to develop new schemes to enhance or to reopen lines and stations.

Avon and Gloucestershire New Stations

New stations in rural areas have tended to require capital grants from local authorities. Avon County Council contributed towards the costs of a new station at Yate, north of Bristol. The area had seen significant housing development over the previous twenty five years. On the same Gloucester to Bristol line, Gloucestershire County Council assisted in the construction of a new station serving Cam and Dursley, where the population had expanded.

[1] *This includes all Saver tickets, unrestricted standard class returns (where no Saver ticket exists), standard weekly season tickets, and, in commuter areas, all standard season tickets and standard single tickets.*

Penistone Line Partnership

The Penistone Line Partnership shows how volunteer-led groups can promote the use of their local railways. The line runs between Huddersfield and Sheffield serving several rural communities. Members of the partnership have been working closely with the various district councils, South and West Yorkshire Passenger Transport Executives (PTE) and Regional Railways North East as well as the parish councils which lie along the route. They have produced a leaflet for visitors and residents promoting attractions and special events which are accessible by train. In conjunction with students from Huddersfield University Studios Department, they have produced a video which is sold to raise more funds. The Partnership is developing ideas for refurbishment of station buildings along the line for community and business use. This includes a bicycle hire shop sponsored by the Rural Development Commission, Countryside Commission and Kirklees District Council. The local Women's Institute are developing a station garden at Stocksmoor. Evening train trips along the line with live jazz and folk music and a real ale bar have been very popular. Local ramblers lead regular guided walks from various stations along the line. The feasibility of running a bus-link to the popular tourist town of Holmfirth is also being examined in conjunction with Holme Valley Parish Council and West Yorkshire PTE. In the longer term, the Partnership hope to raise funding for a development officer.

Future changes in population and development patterns may lead to a reappraisal of the viability of transport routes, such as canal and rail routes which are currently uneconomic. To keep options open for the future, we will encourage planning authorities to consider all potential transport uses of disused transport routes, including use as cycle routes, pedestrian paths and bridleways. Where such potential exists, planning authorities should ensure that these routes are not severed by buildings and non-transport land uses, other than in exceptional circumstances.

HEALTH AND SOCIAL CARE

Over the last five years, both the National Health Service and (NHS) local authority social services have undergone profound changes. These changes have led to improvements in services for people in rural areas, where people have much the same social and health care needs as their counterparts living in towns and cities.

The development of the internal market, the establishment of General Practitioner (GP) fundholding as a major force for change, the community care reforms and the "Health of the Nation" initiative have all changed the way that health and social care are provided. The recently announced expansion of the GP Fundholding Scheme is a very significant step towards a primary care-led NHS, in which decisions about the purchasing and provision of health care are taken as close to patients as possible.

We are committed to building on these improvements in health care across the country, and to ensuring that rural areas share in the benefits. We will encourage the flexible delivery of health care in ways which respond to the needs of rural patients.

Handbook of Good Practice in Rural Areas

The Department of Health will produce a handbook of good practice for health and social care in rural areas, and this will be disseminated widely to health authorities, NHS trusts, General Practitioners and social services departments. It will give examples of where local action has been taken to develop new ways of working and delivering services.

Primary Care

General Practice

Most health care is provided through primary care, especially by GPs. We recognise that rural doctors can have smaller practices, based in more than one location and may therefore need additional financial support. A number of allowances are payable to support GPs in rural areas. The Rural Practice Payments scheme, for example, reflects the costs and pressures of practice in more sparsely populated areas. Other allowances aimed at rural GPs include help with the employment of an associate doctor, inducement payments to encourage doctors to practise in sparsely populated areas and help to meet the cost of a locum in order to attend training courses.

GP Fundholding

GP fundholding has brought major benefits in rural areas, enabling doctors to develop innovative ways of working which bring services closer to patients. Rural doctors have been particularly quick to take advantage of the opportunities: 11 out of the 19 Family Health Services Authorities with over 50% of their population registered with fundholding practices are shire counties and include substantial rural populations. A recent report by the National Audit Office on GP fundholding identified a wide range of benefits for patients, including reduced waiting times and a wider range of services in the practice. For example:

- over 60% are providing physiotherapy in the practice;

- over 50% are holding consultant outreach clinics, where patients enjoy reduced travel and waiting times and are seen more quickly in a familiar environment.

Pocklington Group Practice

The Pocklington Group Practice in North Yorkshire has introduced on-site outpatient clinics for psychiatry, geriatrics, gynaecology, dermatology and general surgery. Previously, patients had to travel 13 miles or more by bus or car to attend the nearest hospital outpatient clinics. The practice premises are also being used as a base for community psychiatric nursing, clinical psychology, community midwives and an alcohol advisory service.

Information Technology

The use of information technology will increasingly help to overcome problems of distance. The Department of Health's "Information Management and Technology (IM&T) Strategy" encourages all NHS organisations to share information and integrate information systems in order to improve communication and information processing. For rural GPs the main benefits will be direct communications with other parts of the NHS, for example with consultants to whom they have referred patients. They will be able to transmit patient data and diagnostic information more quickly.

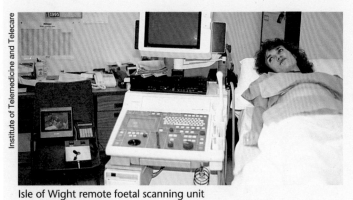

Institute of Telemedicine and Telecare

Isle of Wight remote foetal scanning unit

St. Mary's Hospital

An example of new technology helping people in rural areas is provided by St Mary's hospital on the Isle of Wight which has a remote foetal ultrasound scanning unit. Expectant mothers no longer need to travel long distances to the hospital to have their unborn babies' hearts monitored.

Nursing in Primary Care

Since 1986, the Department of Health has been developing the role of community nursing. Nurse prescribing enables the district nurse to prescribe for patients from a limited list of medicines. This frees the GP and enables nurses making visits to prescribe for patients in their own homes. The scheme is being tested in eight pilot sites around the country involving approximately 60 nurses in GP fundholding practices. Half of these pilots are in rural areas, where patients are now able to obtain their medication much more quickly. If the pilot scheme proves successful in providing genuine benefits for patients, it will be extended and will cover more GP practices in rural areas.

Pharmacists

It is important that people living in rural areas should be able to get their NHS prescriptions dispensed without too much difficulty. Most medium-sized towns and villages have a pharmacy and some of these organise a collection and delivery service. Special payments are available under the Essential Small Pharmacy Scheme to help small pharmacies stay in business where they are more than one kilometre from the next nearest pharmacy.

In addition, doctors are also allowed to dispense to patients living in rural areas in certain circumstances. We are keeping the rules that govern dispensing by doctors and pharmacies in rural areas under careful review, to ensure that patients continue to enjoy reasonable access to a dispensing service.

Secondary Care

Secondary care - the care provided by hospitals - is traditionally concentrated in towns and cities. It is not possible for all services to be provided everywhere. A number of factors have led to the development of larger centres for some services. Services for less common conditions, services which require a lot of high technology equipment or those for which clinical outcomes are better when a specialist sees a large number of patients, are best located in towns and cities. These and other factors, along with the focus in the 1960s and 1970s on building District General Hospitals in towns to serve large catchment areas, have created difficulties for some people in remote areas in gaining access to hospital services.

However, one of the current trends within the NHS is towards new and enhanced roles for traditional cottage or community hospitals. GP fundholding is encouraging this trend by giving GPs the purchasing power to develop local facilities and services. In the past community hospitals have for the most part provided respite care and rehabilitation services, mainly for elderly people. Now many are also offering diagnostic services, day surgery and out-patients clinics provided by visiting consultants, minor conditions services and terminal care closer to the patient's home. Many offer a wide range of low-tech services for rural communities, staffed mainly by nurses, with medical support usually provided by local GPs. This is a very positive development for rural communities.

Community Hospitals

Within Anglia and Oxford Region there are a number of local plans to develop the rôle of community hospitals in a range of ways, and many small local hospitals are already well established. Oxfordshire is developing its large network of community hospitals in Burford, Chipping Norton, Witney and elsewhere. Northamptonshire is considering developing more local services with Brackley voluntary hospital and local GPs. In Suffolk, modern community hospitals are being developed on the sites of old hospitals in Newmarket and Sudbury while partnership with local people has led to extensive building and equipping at the Community Hospital in Aldeburgh.

One of the dangers inherent in developing smaller community hospitals to carry out work previously undertaken in larger units is that of isolation from centres of excellence. In order to help health authorities, GP fundholders, clinicians and NHS trusts overcome these difficulties, the Department of Health has asked the Medical and Nursing and Midwifery Standing Advisory Committees jointly to prepare guidelines which will help small units to maintain high standards. These guidelines will be made widely available.

Ambulance Services

The remoteness of many rural areas makes it more difficult for ambulance services to provide the high standard of service that we would expect in less remote areas. The Department of Health recognised this in the Patient's Charter by setting slightly less rigorous standards for ambulance response times in rural areas. However, it is notable that many ambulance services in rural areas have exceeded the Patient's Charter standard and, through innovative ways of working, have made major improvements to accident and emergency services for people in remote areas.

We recognise that there are still issues to be addressed, and for this reason the Department of Health, with the Ambulance Service, is currently addressing the difficulties of getting faster help to immediately life-threatening conditions in rural areas. A discussion document with proposals for consultation in this area was published in July 1995.

Cumbria Ambulance NHS Trust

Cumbria Rural Ambulance

Rural Ambulance Service

Cumbria Ambulance Service is using innovative ways to improve its service in rural areas. The introduction of a telemetry system enables vital data to be transmitted from the ambulance to the receiving hospital. This enables early diagnosis of the patient's condition to be made by medical staff who can inform paramedics of the appropriate treatment to provide en route. It also permits hospital staff to prepare for the reception of the patient. With distances of 30 miles or more to the nearest Accident and Emergency Department or Intensive Treatment Unit, telemetry is an important development which will underpin the delivery of quality health care to people in rural communities.

East Anglia Ambulance NHS Trust has issued telephone stickers to people living in rural areas so that if they need an ambulance they can quote their grid reference to ensure a rapid response even to the most distant places.

Health in the Countryside

Our "Health of the Nation" initiative aims to improve the general health of the population, by developing strategies to address five key areas: Coronary Heart Disease and Stroke; Cancers; Mental Illness; HIV/AIDS and Sexual Health; and Accidents. In addition to Government action, local people are taking the initiative, and alliances between different organisations in the countryside are being developed to meet the Health of the Nation targets.

Locally led Initiatives in Rural Areas

These include "Partners for Health" - where health authorities work alongside other local groups to develop initiatives. One winner in the Health Alliance Awards was the Shropshire-based Set In Rural Isolation, a partnership which has helped to reduce the number of suicides in farming and rural communities and which is linked to the Rural Stress Initiative, the national alliance which itself was highly commended in the awards.

The UK Health For All Network has recently set up a rural subgroup and is building up a database of good practice, funded by the Department of Health, as well as developing information networks and a newsletter.

There is a high rate of suicides in rural areas, particularly among farmers and vets. The Department of Health funds and works in partnership with voluntary organisations which help people in rural areas with mental health problems, including the Samaritans. A video, "The Last Straw", has been produced for Samaritans volunteers, which highlights the special difficulties faced by those living and working in the countryside.

Health Authorities

One of the most important rôles of health authorities is to assess the needs of the local population and to purchase care to meet those needs. This means that the type and quality of the health service available is no longer dependent on what is provided in the local hospital, but is matched to local needs. As a result, new and more innovative ways of providing services closer to local people's homes are being developed in rural areas.

Northumberland Health Authority

Northumberland Health Authority has replaced some inpatient services in Hexham Memorial Hospital with a range of community-based staff, local day care services and NHS residential facilities, improving access to services for people living in remote areas.

From April 1996, district health authorities and family health services authorities will combine to form new bodies to be known as Health Authorities. Bringing together the two organisations responsible for local health services will enable all types of health care - primary, community and acute (secondary) - to be coordinated in a way which is much more sensitive to local needs.

The Department of Health is also looking at existing ways of allocating funds to health authorities in rural areas and whether sparsity affects the need for community health services, their cost, and the costs of providing other health services. If it transpires that rurality has a significant effect on the cost of health care, or that it is one of the factors driving the need for community health services, we will take this into account in deciding how to allocate resources to Health Authorities.

Social and Community Care

Community Care

Community care aims to ensure that vulnerable people receive the support they need to enable them to live as independently as possible in their own homes or in homely settings in the community. The community care reforms have put users at the centre of a new system for delivering social care services. By encouraging diversity of provision, we aim to ensure that users continue to have choice, underpinned by the development of local community care charters.

We recognise that community care needs to be tailored to local circumstances. Our advice to local authorities about the preparation of community care plans and local community care charters emphasises the need to take account of rural circumstances. Nevertheless, work by the National Council of Voluntary Organisations has shown that few local authorities have an explicit rural strategy in their community care plans. Of course, rural communities and others have a rôle to play locally in urging them to adopt one but we will soon be issuing new guidance on Community Care Plans, which will include the importance of addressing the particular needs of rural areas.

Government Initiatives

Our reforms are already bringing improvements to community care services. We are taking further action to build on this success and will take account of rural circumstances in doing so.

The Department of Health is funding the "Caring for People Who Live at Home" initiative, which was launched in 1992. The initiative aims to stimulate developments which:

- increase the range of services for people living at home by encouraging the independent sector;

- reflect users' and carers' needs;

- improve services including respite care which might help avoid people being admitted to residential care.

Of the participating authorities, six - Cambridgeshire, Devon, Essex, Gloucestershire, North Yorkshire and Shropshire - are involved in stimulating services which cover rural areas. These include shopping and delivery services in Devon and Gloucestershire, outreach day centres in Essex and Gloucestershire, and village warden schemes in Cambridgeshire.

We supported the Carers (Recognition and Services) Act during its passage through Parliament in 1995. The Act will help all carers who provide care on a regular and substantial basis by entitling them to an assessment on request of their ability to provide and continue to provide care. The results must be taken into account when decisions are made about provision for the cared-for person. Policy and practice guidance on the Act will be available and this will highlight issues for rural carers.

We have included a further £30 million in community care funding in 1995-96 to encourage further development of home care and respite care services. This will benefit people living in rural areas who wish to remain in their own homes as well as isolated single carers who look after vulnerable people at home and who need to take a break.

Local Initiatives

Many of the most exciting community care initiatives are locally led. Carers' helplines, developed locally and based on local knowledge of needs and services, can play a useful rôle in rural areas, helping to address some of the problems of isolation experienced by carers living in more remote areas.

Information for Carers

In Somerset the 'SIGNPOSTS' Freefone number provides a valuable source of information about health and social care for service users and carers. Launched in September 1993, it provided advice to 3,000 enquirers in its first year. It complements a range of other information services available through social services offices, GP surgeries and voluntary agencies, including a computer database of disability information.

Nottinghamshire Social Services Department employs carers' support workers - a number of whom are based in rural areas - specifically to address the isolation which carers are prone to in rural areas.

EDUCATION

Pre-School Education

All children deserve the best possible start to their educational lives. Our recent announcement of a voucher system to fund pre-school provision will give all four year olds a good quality pre-school place for three terms before compulsory school age, in rural as in other areas.

The parents of all four year olds will be given a voucher worth around £1,100 which they will be able to exchange for a good quality pre-school place in the state, private or voluntary sector. Parental demand, with purchasing power in the form of a voucher, will stimulate the private and voluntary sectors to provide more places. This opens up exciting opportunities for new partnerships to develop, involving the private, voluntary and state sectors, and for the identification of innovatory solutions to improve access to pre-school provision in rural areas to be found. These solutions could well have important lessons for the cost-effective provision of the subsequent stages of education in rural areas.

The scheme will be introduced in two phases. The first phase, in a number of areas, will start in April 1996 and the scheme will be introduced throughout the United Kingdom in April 1997. We are keen to ensure that rural areas are fully represented in phase 1.

Rural Schools

Some 4,000 of England's 19,000 primary schools are in rural areas. Their contribution to the quality of village life is valued not only for the education they provide for the children, but also for the focus they provide for the community they serve, the sense of security they bring to the children, and the balance they give to village life.

Of course, rural schools tend to be smaller than average. In the past there has tended to be a belief that small schools could not provide as good an education as their larger counterparts. Early findings from the first year of the Office of Standards in Education (OFSTED) inspection do not support that view.

Ingoldisthorpe, Norfolk. Church of England first school.

Based on a small sample of primary schools these findings indicate that pupils in the schools with fewer than 100 pupils on roll, most of which are rural, achieve standards which are slightly higher than those achieved by pupils in the larger schools. Overall, the quality of learning tends to be slightly better in the small rather than the larger schools. On a wide range of comparisons concerned with the quality of education provision, small schools are rated rather more favourably than larger ones.

The relatively high cost of maintaining small rural schools, particularly when combined with significant proportions of surplus places, had led to 350 closures over the last 12 years. But the rate has been going down: just 80 have been closed since 1990. Many small rural primary schools are of good quality, popular with parents and within easy reach of the children they serve. All the more reason for any proposal for closure of such a school to be scrutinized very carefully indeed before a final decision is reached by the Secretary of State. So, while we continue to press authorities to remove surplus places where practicable in the interests of maximizing cost-effectiveness we have emphasised that the Secretary of State:

- will not normally approve the closure of a school where the alternative schooling on offer is not of at least equivalent quality;

- weighs very carefully the consequences of closure proposals, including for example, the impact on children's journeys to school, as well as the effect on the wider community;

- accepts the need to preserve accessibility of schooling for young children as a justification for retaining surplus places.

Where provision is being rationalised through the amalgamation of a county and a Church school, there is often a desire on the part of the local community for the new school to retain the Church connection. Such an option is possible under existing legislation, and the Secretary of State would welcome such proposals where there is strong feeling within the community that this is the best way forward.

Enhancing Quality

There is much rural schools can do - and are doing - to ensure that they provide an education of good quality. As highlighted in a 1991 Department report[1] on rural schools, collaborative clustering arrangements can be particularly beneficial. These range from informal contacts between staff to, most effectively, systematic co-operation in curricular provision, including the shared use of teachers and materials.

The Education Act 1993 extends the options open to small schools by enabling them to apply jointly for grant-maintained status as a cluster, operating either under a single governing body, or a joint committee of governing bodies. The aim is to put GM status within reach of schools that might otherwise lack the confidence to go it alone. This is an important opportunity for rural schools, because while they tend to have strong links with the communities they serve, self government gives schools great flexibility to respond quickly and effectively to local needs.

[1] *Rural Schools Curriculum Enhancement National Evaluation (SCENE) Project published in 1991 by the Department for Education and Science. ISBN No. 0 85522 406 1.*

Community Use

Schools can make a valuable contribution to strengthening community life in rural areas by making their premises available for community activities such as sport, adult education and parish meetings. For its part, the Department for Education and Employment supports the use made of schools for "out-of-school" clubs through its £45 million "Out-of-School Childcare" initiative.

"Out-of-School" Clubs: All Saints Primary, Winfarthing, Norfolk.

In 1992 the head teacher started an after-school club in response to the lack of facilities locally and at the request of parents. A grant from the local Training and Enterprise Council was used to buy play equipment, and advice and guidance on getting started was provided by an out of school organisation. The club is managed by the head and staffed by the school's welfare assistant. Opening times are 3.30 to 5.30 pm, Monday to Friday. The club is not an extension of school activities, but rather a place for children to play and relax. Fees are £2 per session or £8.75 per week. Any profits are ploughed back into the club and used to buy more play equipment.

Charlotte MacPherson/Environment Picture Library

New Communications Technologies in Education

New communications technologies have enormous potential for education in sparsely populated areas. We jointly published a consultation paper[1], Superhighways for Education, in April 1995 to draw attention to the possibilities. Progress towards defining the uses which rural communities can make of advanced communications technologies - including distance learning - is being made under the Kington Connected Community Project in Herefordshire, supported by a number of sponsors including BT and Apple Computers, and by the Government.

In Northamptonshire, the Department for Education and Employment, in partnership with the Rural Development Commission, the Local Education Authority and commercial sponsors, is supporting a pilot project which delivers in-service training in science to teachers in a cluster of six primary schools, by means of electronic mail telephone links. This project will have important lessons for the potential for such services to provide specialist teaching in rural primary schools.

Information Technology is having a significant impact on the provision made by Further Education Colleges. Most colleges have open learning or "drop-in" centres where students can work at their own pace with computer based learning materials. These materials are increasingly available through "distance learning" to students who cannot attend a college either on a regular basis or at all. Distance learning is set to grow in importance to the benefit of students based in rural areas.

[1] Superhighways for Education 1995, HMSO, ISBN No 0 11 270898 6

All these issues, including the contribution that new communications technologies can make to lifelong learning, will be explored further in a paper to be published in the Autumn of 1995 announcing the outcomes of the consultation on Superhighways for Education. At the same time will be announced the pilot projects to be evaluated under the initiative, several of which are expected to have implications for education in rural areas.

SHOPS AND POST OFFICES

Shops

The Nature of the Village Shop

Village shop, Yorkshire

The village shop is often the focal point of a small community and frequently provides a lifeline for members of the community who are unable to get to town on a regular basis. It often acts as post office, newsagent and grocers; it may sell books and videos or take in dry cleaning. The entrepreneurial shopkeeper can provide a range of goods and services in a location where they would otherwise be unavailable. Loss of the village shop can therefore be a serious blow to village life.

Recent Trends

The number of retail outlets in Great Britain has declined from 577,000 in 1961 to about 319,000 in 1992. This decline has particularly affected village shops and small retail outlets in town centres, although there has been an increase in farm shops.

This decline is attributable to a broader change in lifestyles. More people now own cars, more women go to work and consumers demand more sophisticated products. People are less likely to use the local greengrocer or the butcher on a daily basis to shop for food. They often prefer to drive to a supermarket once a week to choose from a much wider range of goods. Prices are likely to be lower there too.

Planning Policy

We wish to maintain the vitality and viability of town and village centres. Planning Policy Guidance note 7 *The Countryside and the Rural Economy* advises local authorities that it is important to maintain a healthy rural economy and that this should be taken into account when considering applications for the change of use of existing shops into private dwellings. Through Planning Policy Guidance note 6 *Town Centres and Retail Developments* we insist that local authorities have regard to the possible impact on village shops of proposed new retail developments.

Business Rating

Many rural shopkeepers feel that the burden of non-domestic rates is a significant threat to their continued viability. There is supporting evidence in recent research carried out for the Department of the Environment. This shows that, while for most businesses rate bills are small in relation to total turnover, they impose a more substantial burden on the smallest businesses, particularly retail ones.

We see no case for subsidising the general run of shops which fail to attract sufficient custom to remain viable. However, the small general store or post office in a rural village has a special social function. It often provides an invaluable, and irreplaceable, service for local people without cars or ready access to public transport. Its demise would be a severe blow to the community.

We therefore intend to introduce, at a suitable legislative opportunity, a new rate relief scheme targeted specifically on general stores and post offices in villages. We will consult widely on the technical details, but meanwhile we envisage that, to qualify for consideration, the shop would need to satisfy a number of conditions as to location, size, purpose and importance to the local community. It would not however be necessary to demonstrate that the ratepayer was suffering hardship.

Since it will be some time before the new scheme can come into effect, we propose in the meantime to review the way the existing scheme of hardship relief works. Local authorities already have discretion to reduce or remit the payment of rates, taking account of the interests of local council taxpayers, where they are satisfied that the ratepayer would sustain hardship if they did not do so. Guidance issued to billing authorities in 1990 and 1992 drew attention to village shops as potentially deserving cases, and commended guidelines which had been adopted by Test Valley District Council on the application of hardship relief. The Test Valley guidelines aimed to ensure that general stores were maintained for the benefit of the local rural community. They recognised that in such communities the loss of the village shop could well be more serious than the loss of a small shop in a town or city.

Nonetheless, the policies and practices of individual authorities seem to vary greatly. The total amount of hardship relief given is very small and many local authorities in rural areas give none at all. We therefore intend to review the way authorities are operating the scheme now, identify examples of good practice and issue fresh guidance to secure a more consistent approach. This will again emphasise the importance for authorities of having clear local policies and procedures on hardship relief, making them widely known and explaining the reasons for the decisions they reach.

Local Action

The Rural Development Commission (RDC) provides assistance and training for village shopkeepers. It provides a network of Retail and Business Advisors, who in 1994/95 made around 570 visits to village shopkeepers. During 1995/96 the RDC will pilot a new retail grant scheme to help shopkeepers invest in modern equipment which is intended to enhance the service they provide and to improve their viability. If this is a success, the RDC will consider introducing a nationwide scheme. Business Links advisory services are also available to all businesses, however small, including village shops.

Local people can play an important part in supporting the village shop. The Rural Community Councils work directly with local communities to identify practical ways of securing the future of the village shop.

We commend the valuable work of organisations such as the RDC, the Rural Community Councils and the Village Retail Services Association in helping to ensure the survival of the village shop. We will encourage closer working between these organisations.

The National Lottery

Many shops, garages and sub-post offices in rural areas are already selling National Lottery tickets, or will be doing so by the end of 1996 when Camelot will have completed its network of around 40,000 retailers. The Director General of the National Lottery has directed Camelot to ensure that there is at least one Lottery retailer in every local authority area, but, in practice, it is likely that provision will be more widespread. With ticket sales continuing to run ahead of expectations, and retailers entitled to a commission of 5% on all sales, it is clear that this will bring considerable additional revenue to shopkeepers across the country. In some cases this might make the difference between a shop having to close or remaining open.

The Post Office

Serving the Rural Community

The Post Office has an unrivalled nationwide network of 19,500 offices across the United Kingdom, about half of which are in rural areas. Like village shops, with which they are often linked, rural post offices fulfil a vital function as meeting places and sources of information on local services and activities.

Michael Allwood-Coppin/National Trust Photographic Library

Allerford Post Office, Somerset

Post offices provide a wide range of services which are particularly valuable in the remoter rural areas and represent a lifeline for less mobile members of the community. As well as selling stamps, collecting parcels and offering a variety of other commercial services, they distribute benefits for the Department of Social Security and offer bill payment and savings facilities.

Recent Developments

Following the recent Post Office review, we have reaffirmed our commitment to a nationwide letter and parcel service, featuring daily delivery of mail to every address in the country. We will maintain a nationwide network of Post Offices and it will continue to cost the same to post a letter no matter where it is posted or where it is sent throughout the United Kingdom.

We have agreed to grant Post Office Counters Limited (POCL) greater freedom to take on new clients and offer new services, opening up exciting opportunities for new areas of business and strengthening the commercial viability of our post offices. The Department of Trade and Industry's Green Paper *The Future of Postal Services* introduced new guidelines for the diversification of POCL's activities. POCL has responded swiftly and is already the largest national *bureau de change* chain, with foreign currency exchange facilities at nearly 19,000 outlets. It is also the largest retail outlet for the National Lottery.

There has been a decline in the number of post offices in recent years. During 1994/95, there was a net reduction of 112. POCL's objective is that there should be no net closures of post offices. Where it is no longer possible to maintain a full-time post office, POCL will try to introduce a part-time, community post office. Community post offices are a last resort, and ideally a temporary measure, but they do provide a valuable service, ensuring access to the full range of post office services. There are now about 1,850 community post offices in England and Wales. The provision of a community post office depends on individuals' goodwill and many are in unusual places such as village pubs and local schools.

The Swan, Little Totham, Essex

The Swan is a seventeenth century pub which was originally a coaching inn. Situated in Little Totham, in Essex, the Swan is the only pub in the village of 325 residents and is very successful. Part of the pub has been leased out for the past four years to run the local community post office. When the village shop, which housed the original post office, closed down, action had to be taken to keep the village post office open, and so it was moved to the pub. There is a post box emptied daily. The post office counter is open two mornings a week. It provides all services except issuing road tax licences and has proved extremely useful for local residents particularly old age pensioners.

Automation of benefit payments

People who receive social security benefits or pensions will continue to have the choice of payment direct into their bank or building society accounts by Automated Credit Transfer or in cash via their local post office. We have however decided to replace order books and giro cheques with plastic cards which can be used to obtain payments at post office counters.

The Benefits Agency and POCL are working together on a major project to automate each post office counter and issue benefit payment cards. All automated counter points will be linked to a computer system which the clerk will access using an authenticated benefit payment card. The customer will receive social security or war pensions payment and a copy of a signed receipt from the clerk. Introduction of this system will begin in 1996 and, as this is a major task, will take two to three years to complete.

The automation and benefit card programme will provide a more secure, efficient and economic service to customers which will continue the recent improvements in the standards of service provided both by POCL and the Benefits Agency. Automation will also provide scope for extending existing services such as payment of utility or other bills and will attract clients who wish to transact large number of payments with a high level of security. We will encourage the Post Office to take advantage of automation to deliver new services to its customers, such as the sale of travel and theatre tickets, insurance and banking services.

Information Technology

Business and private use of forms of instant communication such as faxes, e-mail and the video link is expanding rapidly. Although the cost of the equipment necessary to make use of these new modes of communication is falling, it is unlikely that every home will be fully equipped in the foreseeable future. This suggests that there will be a continuing need for publicly available facilities. We will be encouraging the Post Office to stay in the forefront of communication and information technology through the development of business centres which will offer the latest IT capabilities to its customers, along with already familiar services such as printing and fax transmission.

BENEFITS

The Benefits Agency has undertaken a number of initiatives to counter the problem of access to benefits offices in rural areas. it. Each local area is able to adopt its own strategy for serving most effectively the needs of the local community. This may include the use of benefits buses, mobile information units which travel around the local area providing benefits advice. Advice surgeries in village halls are another useful innovation.

The Benefits Agency

The Benefits Agency , an executive agency of the Department of Social Security, is responsible for the majority of social security benefits - the exceptions being unemployment benefit (dealt with by the Employment Service) and housing and council tax benefits (dealt with by local authorities). Unemployment benefit, along with Income Support for unemployed people, will be replaced by the Job Seekers Allowance in October 1996.

One of the Benefits Agency's Benefits Buses

East Yorkshire Benefits Bus

The East Yorkshire benefit bus was launched in January 1993 and serves a 1,300 square mile rural area five days a week. The bus service is planned and advertised weeks in advance to ensure maximum take up of the service.

People in rural areas who experience difficulty in travelling to their local office to make a claim may telephone or write to obtain the claim forms and then submit them by post. They are asked to attend in person only in exceptional circumstances. If an interview is necessary, travelling expenses may be reimbursed, and if the customer is unable to attend the benefit office, a home visit can be arranged.

The Benefits Agency recognises that much can be learned by sharing ideas and experiences and is encouraging an improved rural service by widely disseminating examples of best practice service delivery in rural areas. In order to facilitate this the Benefits Agency has held a number of conferences aimed at identifying the problems rural people face in obtaining advice and making claims for benefit. It is looking at ways in which these can be overcome. The results of these conferences have been compiled into a report which has been distributed to managers.

LIBRARIES

Public libraries are a valuable community resource. As well as books and other materials they enable users to access a wide range of community and other information and can also contribute to economic and social regeneration. They provide an important gateway to local authority services.

Local authorities have a statutory duty to provide a comprehensive and efficient public library service throughout their area. Authorities which cover rural areas face particular challenges in carrying out this duty. Many authorities serve rural areas by supplementing their fixed library network with mobile libraries. Some are also investigating more innovative approaches to library provision, for example by taking advantage of information technology to operate library services through local shops.

Suffolk County Council's Saxmundham-based mobile library outside Rendlesham church in East Suffolk

Rural Development Commission

Norfolk County Council

The Library Service in Norfolk has introduced a pilot scheme under which libraries have been established in three village shops. These are all in areas of scattered population with poor communications. The Library Service has received support from the Rural Development Commission, the Department of National Heritage and several charitable organisations. Each shop contains a selection of paperback books. Users are able to see which books are available at other libraries in Norfolk and to place orders, using an on-line terminal in the shop.

We published a report on library services in rural areas in July 1993. The report, prepared by the Library and Information Services Council, emphasised that people in rural areas have a right to receive the same quality of library and information services as those in cities and towns.

Among other recommendations, the report called for changes to the sparsity indicator in Standard Spending Assessments for local authorities and we have improved the indicator's sensitivity from 1994/95. The report also looked at the Government's Public Library Development Incentive Scheme (PLDIS) and the role of performance indicators. The PLDIS applies as much in rural areas as in urban areas and we are currently considering the future of the scheme. Similarly, the Audit Commission's library performance indicators apply equally in rural areas. For example, local authorities have to provide information about the opening hours of libraries and the number of mobile libraries. The public will be able to make year-on-year comparisons of opening hours, mobile libraries, use of libraries by the public, and expenditure.

Public Library Development Incentive Scheme

Past awards under the Public Library Development Incentive Scheme have included a grant to Somerset Library Service to help create a business information service tailored to the needs of industries in the agricultural, horticultural and tourism sectors. An award was also made to the Golden Valley Information Project in Hereford and Worcester which investigated the provision of networked information services in remote rural areas.

CRIME AND POLICING

Whether we live in the town or the country, our sense of well-being is directly influenced by the extent to which we feel secure from threats to our person or property. Many people choose to live in the countryside because the chances of becoming a victim of crime are lower than in a town or a city. The risk of burglary is around half the national average and the risk of robbery and theft from the person about four fifths of the national average. Nevertheless there is increasing anxiety in the countryside at what is perceived as a rising incidence of crime.

Levels of crime have risen in rural areas as well as urban areas in recent years. However, the rise was from a much lower base than in urban areas. Over the past two years there has been a very welcome reduction of 10% in recorded crime across the country. This benefit has been felt in rural areas and some of the largest decreases in recorded crime have been in the most rural of police force areas, such as Norfolk.

The Nature of Rural Crime and Policing

The types of crime committed in the countryside are generally the same as those committed in urban centres, including burglary and theft for example. There are, however, some differences. Farmers may suffer from animal rustling, trespass or theft of farm equipment and roofing slates. The theft of valuables from cars parked at countryside beauty spots is a particular problem.

Police Authorities are responsible for publishing annual policing plans for their area, setting out the priorities for policing, including local objectives, in consultation with Chief Constables and the local community. Chief Constables are responsible for the deployment of resources on the ground.

Many police forces have large rural areas and have mounted initiatives to tackle crime in those areas. Nevertheless rural communities, particularly those in remoter areas, can suffer the twin problems of a less obvious police presence and longer response times to emergency calls. It is therefore particularly important for those who live in rural areas to act as the eyes and ears of the police.

All forces are required to set target times for responding to incidents that require an immediate response. Forces can set different target times for urban and rural areas, to reflect local conditions, and performance is monitored against these targets.

The Government's Strategy

Our strategy for tackling crime in rural areas is based on crime prevention. Crime prevention can include straightforward measures such as fitting window and door locks but it also includes Neighbourhood Watch schemes and installing closed circuit television systems in some areas. Making crime more difficult to commit and increasing the likelihood of being seen while committing crime will make criminals think twice.

Devon and Cornwall Constabulary

In small communities crime prevention is best carried out through individual responsibility, partnership and local action. We believe that parish councils and local volunteers, working with the police, can have a real impact.

Local people often have the best solutions to local problems and that is why our overall approach to improving safety and security in rural areas concentrates on providing the right framework for individual initiatives.

Crime Prevention

Many crimes are opportunistic. Simple crime prevention measures, such as having a car immobiliser fitted and remembering to lock doors, can help prevent crime. Crime prevention can also help to address the fear of crime.

As part of a general programme of advice in support of crime prevention measures, the 1994 Department of the Environment and Welsh Office circular *Planning Out Crime* gives practical advice to local authorities, developers and designers about planning considerations relevant to crime prevention. The Home Office leaflet *The Big Steal Is On* gives practical advice to farmers on how to make their farms more secure. Some 335,000 copies of the leaflet and 29,500 copies of a poster have been distributed via local police Crime Prevention Officers. Other bodies such as the National Farmers' Union have also published useful advice.

A recent development in crime prevention is the use of closed circuit television (CCTV) surveillance systems. We are encouraging their use to monitor high streets, shopping centres, car parks, industrial estates and other areas. As well as helping to reduce levels of crime, the presence of the cameras also helps people to feel more secure.

The majority of CCTV systems have so far been introduced in large towns and cities but they can be equally effective in smaller centres of population. The recent £5 million CCTV Challenge Competition focused on promoting CCTV schemes in these areas. The winning bids included a number from rural market towns and villages.

The Criminal Justice and Public Order Act 1994 contains a provision which gives a specific power to local authorities to spend money on CCTV schemes in their areas in partnership with the private sector and others. Planning regulations were relaxed in June 1995 to allow cameras to be installed in most cases without the need for express planning permission. The Home Office has also produced a guidance booklet *CCTV - Looking Out For You* which has been distributed widely to those who may be thinking of setting up a CCTV system to help combat crime.

In 1988 we established Crime Concern as an independent crime prevention organisation. Crime Concern receives £500,000 per year in grant aid to enable it carry out its work, which includes setting up crime prevention and community safety partnerships, developing specific crime prevention initiatives and providing training for people involved in community safety. In partnership with Gloucestershire Constabulary, Crime Concern hosted the first National Rural Crime Prevention Conference in 1994. The conference considered ways of preventing crime in rural areas and encouraged the spread of best practice.

It is important to ensure that young people do not become constant offenders. In rural areas, some people can feel threatened by young people who may be loitering because there are no local after-school activities. Providing youth clubs and youth activities can stop young people from drifting into crime.

The Rural Development Commission and a number of local partners have commissioned Crime Concern to undertake surveys of young people to look at their involvement in and their concerns about crime. The surveys also asked young people for their ideas on how to reduce crime. The results of these Youth Surveys will be published later in 1995. They will help the police and local authorities to be more responsive to young people's concerns.

Nottinghamshire Community Safety Challenge

Nottinghamshire County Council has introduced challenge funding for schemes to prevent youth crime in partnership with the Rural Development Commission and Nottinghamshire Drug Prevention Team. Proposals involved parish councils, neighbourhood groups and young people. One of the schemes supported was Selston Mobile Information/Youth Project, set up because of increasing youth crime. The Project's Information Bus visits two evenings a week with both an information worker and local youth worker. The scheme is expanding to include mini-bus excursions for young people.

Local Authorities

Local authorities have an important part to play in preventing crime in a variety of ways including the installation of appropriate street lighting. We are encouraging them to develop community safety strategies which give specific attention to the needs of rural areas. Some 220 local community safety partnerships have already been formed across the country, many of which address crime problems in rural areas.

Crime Concern will shortly be publishing a guide for parish councils containing practical advice on crime prevention. Support is being provided by the Rural Development Commission and private sector sponsors. We will encourage parish councils to take effective action using their existing powers.

Coningsby Parish Council and Police Station, Lincolnshire

In 1994, the local police force invited the Coningsby Parish Council to share accommodation to make use of a previously unstaffed police station in the village centre. In return for rent-free accommodation, the parish clerk now acts as a contact point for the police, recording details of lost property, dealing with fixed penalty fines, taking crime reports and answering general enquiries.

Although the parish clerk is only paid to work two days per week, the office is now usually open every day because the clerk also works there as a volunteer at other times. There has therefore been a huge increase in the number of hours when the public has access to the police station and links between the council and police have also improved enormously.

The scheme has been a great success and the use of volunteers has been extended to other police stations in the area.

We wish to enable parish councils to work more closely with the police. An example is contributing towards the costs of recruiting, training and equipping local neighbourhood special constables on duty in the area. We also wish to give them a more specific power to support crime prevention activity, if they think this is appropriate. This could be achieved by extending to parish councils the powers currently available to district and county councils.[1] Legislation would be necessary to enable parish councils to carry out these modest but important functions if they wish in addition to their other activities. We invite comments on these broad proposals by March 1996, and will discuss these ideas with the Local Authority Associations.[2]

Community Action

We encourage close partnership between the police and the local community. Our "Partners Against Crime" campaign concentrates on three complementary partnerships:

- **Neighbourhood Watch**

- **Neighbourhood Constable**

- **Street Watch.**

There are now 130,000 Neighbourhood Watch schemes throughout England and Wales and more specific watch schemes have also developed, such as Farm Watch, Horse Watch, School Watch and Vehicle Watch. The success of Neighbourhood Watch varies but in some areas the scheme has helped to reduce crime by up to 75%. It is particularly effective in small rural communities where people are more likely to know one another and spot anything out of the ordinary.

We are also encouraging community involvement in crime prevention through volunteer police schemes. Special constables are volunteers who devote part of their time to training and serving as uniformed police constables. They have the same powers as regular police officers. Although there are already over 20,000 special constables in England and Wales we want to see more and have set a target of 30,000 by 1996. To show our commitment to this target we have started a new fund for special constables to support increased recruitment and ensure a good standard of training, equipment and supervision. We have provided £4 million of central Government grant to start the ball rolling but we are looking to increase the fund with local challenge funding from the community and national sponsorship. Central money will also be allocated to police forces where police and community support for these volunteers is highest.

Chiseldon Special Constable

Chiseldon village in Wiltshire has its own special constable. A local resident, he concentrates his duties in Chiseldon and neighbouring villages, working together with the rural policing team. The parish council and four local businesses have equipped him with a mobile telephone to use when on foot patrol.

---

[1] *The relevant powers are contained in S.24 of the Police and Magistrates' Courts Act 1994 and S.163 of the Criminal Justice and Public Order Act 1994.*

[2] *Comments should be sent to Steven Watts, Room N7/16, Department of the Environment, 2 Marsham Street, London, SW1P 3EB.*

Voluntary Policing

Special Constable
A volunteer who gives spare time to train and serve with the police as a constable, wears police uniform, and has the same powers as a regular officer.

Neighbourhood Special Constable
Neighbourhood Special Constables are Special Constables who, with the agreement of the chief officer and in pursuit of the force's policy plan, spend the majority of their duty time on foot patrol and in uniform either alone or as part of a policing team within an agreed neighbourhood or limited area. Some police forces in rural areas prefer to keep the original name of Parish Special Constable. There are over 300 rural communities with a Neighbourhood Special Constable and many forces are reorganising their deployment of specials along community policing lines. In rural communities, Neighbourhood Special Constable schemes are often a three-way partnership between the police, the volunteer and the local parish council. The parish council may provide facilities for the constable to use and give specific advice on local concerns.

The Government has set a target of 1,000 Neighbourhood Special Constables by the end of 1995 and 3,000 by the end of 1996. Many of these will be in rural areas.

Street Watch
Street Watch members are not uniformed and do not have police powers. They are local people who regularly walk a specific route in their community and, if they spot anything, report it to the police. Street Watch Schemes must be set up in consultation with the police and local communities. The Home Office will produce a good practice guide with details of successful schemes.

THE RURAL ENVIRONMENT

Objectives

8 week old triplet otter cubs

The retention of flower-rich hay meadows, one of Britain's rarest and most fragile habitats, is a key objective of the Environmentally Sensitive Area Scheme in many designated areas. Over 22,000 hectares of hay meadows are currently protected under the Scheme

For centuries the English countryside has been a resource for the nation as a whole. This chapter describes something of what is distinctive about our countryside and why it is worth preserving. It explains how we can use the countryside's resources sustainably. It first sets out the objectives which guide our actions. Later sections show how these inform policies for farming and forestry; recreation and public access to land; land use planning; and the sustainable use of other key resources.

In recent years we have seen a new awareness of the importance of environmental issues both here and abroad. Our landscapes and wildlife are finite assets and most people now have far more opportunity to enjoy them than was once the case. Yet the pressures upon the countryside are immense. Intensive farming, building, roads, the spread of towns and villages, and the retail provision for car-borne customers - all these represent demands upon our rural areas.

Yet the countryside is not just ours. It is also the home of much of England's flora and fauna. Mankind's unique position of power brings with it responsibility. Life forms which have evolved over millions of years can be destroyed forever by one thoughtless act on our part.

Some features of our countryside are irreplaceable and must be protected. Ancient woodland, for example, cannot be recovered once developed. However, for most of us, it is the everyday species of plants and animals - the common farmland birds, for example - which give most pleasure, and which are most missed when they are absent. They are all dependent for their survival on the ways in which land is managed across the countryside.

Our National Parks and Areas of Outstanding Natural Beauty are only the most striking examples of a countryside which is full of variety and wonder. This is our inheritance, and it has been preserved by generations of country people who have cared for it. Yet these same generations also scarred it with their mines and factories, their pollution and their extraction. Truly, the countryside "wears man's smudge and shares man's smell".

The countryside supplies many of the natural resources which meet our basic material needs. Its soil and water sustain plant and animal life. Its minerals are used to construct the nation's roads and buildings. Yet we have never been more aware of the limits of non-renewable resources and of the heavy demands which our life style places on them. They need to be managed carefully in order to preserve them for future generations and minimise harm to the environment.

Development ought to be a good word. After all, it is an essential element in human life. Sadly it has acquired a bad name among many who live in the countryside. We need therefore to create an attitude to development which ensures that it enhances or preserves the character of the countryside, its market towns and villages.

Derwent Water and sheep

Development needs to be part of the mix. Protection and preservation alone would turn rural England into a museum. Insensitive development causes more harm but stagnation too is very damaging. The things which most characterise the English countryside are largely the product of human enterprise - villages and towns, much of the landscape, for example all of the Norfolk Broads. Rural communities need to be economically viable if they are to maintain and enhance a countryside so significantly the product of man's work.

South Downs Environmentally Sensitive Area, west from Itford Hill, East Sussex, Sussex Down

Yet development and conservation are not opposites. Wealth creation and environmental quality are increasingly interconnected. In the 21st century environmental quality will offer more economic opportunities than constraints. This is particularly true of tourism and recreation, which depend on a high quality environment to attract visitors. But many other businesses, which bring prosperity and jobs to the countryside, cite environmental quality as a reason for their location in rural areas.

Public Attitudes to the Countryside

In 1995 the Countryside Commission commissioned a survey of public attitudes to the countryside among householders across England. Interviews were conducted with adults living in the countryside, towns, suburbs and inner city areas, and these found that:

- 93% consider that the countryside is valuable to them, whether they visit it or not;

- 91% believe that society has a moral duty to protect the countryside for future generations;

The most common benefits from visiting the countryside were a sense of relaxation and well being (45%), fresh air (36%) and peace and quiet (22%).

The rural environment is a valuable resource which answers many different demands. These demands are not always compatible. Sustainable development not only places on us all a responsibility to manage the countryside in ways that meet present needs without compromising the ability of future generations to meet theirs, it also requires us to reconcile the many competing priorities.

In order to safeguard the future of our countryside, we as a nation have a collective responsibility to:

- conserve the countryside's natural assets, managing them wisely and avoiding irreversible damage wherever possible in order to maintain or enhance their value for generations to come;

- reverse the decline in wildlife, sustaining the wealth of flora and fauna across the countryside and conserving the populations of rare species;

- maintain the diversity of rural landscapes;

- redress the environmental damage of the past and ensure that unavoidable damage in the future is offset wherever possible through other environmental improvements;

- safeguard the quality and particular character of rural towns and villages;

- increase opportunities for people to enjoy the countryside for recreation;

- acknowledge and exploit the interdependence of environmental protection and economic development;

- establish processes at national and local level to reconcile competing demands in an open and accessible manner.

Monitoring and Research

If we are to make sound decisions about the management of the countryside environment, and where necessary change our priorities, we need reliable information about the state of the environment and the many factors which impact on it. **We must therefore base our policies on the best information available, by monitoring trends in the countryside and improving access to this information.**

Measuring bill of bartailed godwit

British Trust for Ornithology

Most of the British Trust for Ornithology's fieldwork is carried out by its 10,000 voluntary members and other bird watchers. The Trust conducts research and surveys of bird populations and their habitats, including long- term monitoring of birds of both inland and coastal wetlands. The Trust also runs the British and Irish bird-ringing scheme which helps to monitor changes in bird populations.

For many years, the Government, our countryside agencies and voluntary bodies have monitored environmental change in the countryside and published the results. *Countryside Survey*[1], published in 1993, recorded changes in common features and habitats which are most likely to influence our experience of the countryside. It recorded a sample stock of countryside features in 1990 and compared them with earlier surveys in 1978 and 1984. Its results showed a broad decline in plant species and habitats across the countryside, especially in lowland areas. The survey provides a firm baseline against which future changes can be assessed. **The Government will carry out a repeat survey in the year 2000 as a way of monitoring the success of our countryside policies.**

[1]*Countryide Survey 1990, Department of the Environment 1993*

Countryside Survey

Countryside Survey involved a field survey of 508 one kilometre squares supplemented by images of the ground obtained by satellite. It was one of the most comprehensive surveys of the British countryside ever completed. It found that:

- between 1984 and 1990 the net length of managed hedgerow decreased by 23%;

- between 1984 and 1990 the area of broadleaved woodland increased by 3%;

- between 1984 and 1990 there was little net change in the overall extent of habitats such as heathland, moorland and bogs, but in some categories, such as meadows, there was a continuing loss of higher quality habitat balanced by a gain of newly created, poorer quality habitat;

- between 1978 and 1990 there were significant losses in lowland areas in the species diversity of arable fields and of semi-improved grasslands which are rich in wild flowers;

- between 1978 and 1990 the species diversity of hedgerows decreased by 8%.

For the future, we need to improve our understanding of countryside change so that policies can anticipate harmful changes and pre-empt them. We will therefore endeavour to:

- interpret observed changes in the countryside, and understand their causes and their significance for wildlife;

- improve methods of forecasting changes in land use and their consequences;

- improve the integration and accessibility of data on the countryside so that better use can be made of it.

The UK "Biodiversity Action Plan", published in 1994, set in train action to improve the coordination and accessibility of existing information on native plants and animals. We will encourage improved coordination at national and local levels so that progress towards the targets for key species and habitats can be monitored.

Biodiversity

Over 170 native species in the United Kingdom are thought to have become extinct in the past 100 years. All our wildlife species, the rare as well as the common, are part of our natural capital. We all share a responsibility to sustain them, and the habitats on which they rely, and to reverse the decline in their populations.

Having signed the Biodiversity Convention at the Earth Summit, the United Kingdom became one of the first countries to produce a biodiversity strategy in January 1994. The Action Plan commits us to:

- seek to conserve and where possible enhance wild species and wildlife habitats;

• ensure that all policy areas respect and integrate these concerns;

• increase public awareness and involvement in conserving biodiversity.

A steering group, with members drawn from national and local government, academic institutions, voluntary organisations, landowners and others, is taking this work forward. It will report before the end of 1995 with proposals for improving the conservation of our most threatened species and habitats. These will include costed targets, for example for re-establishing lowland heathland or increasing the population of booming bitterns. Targets agreed by Government will form the basis of our nature conservation effort over the next two decades.

Shared Responsibility

Most land is owned and managed by private individuals. Practical responsibility for sustainable land management therefore rests primarily with them. Land ownership encourages responsibility. Most land managers and rural entrepreneurs have a personal stake in the quality of the countryside environment. Many have chosen to live and work there because they were attracted to its environment, and farmers have an obvious interest in managing their land wisely and handing it down to their children in good order. We rely on them to act as stewards of England's countryside, using best environmental practice to nurture its quality and wealth of wildlife.

In recent years they have been joined by voluntary organisations and environmental charities who carry out valuable work in the countryside and enjoy widespread public support. Many have grown remarkably in membership and in the scale of their activities. The National Trust and the Royal Society for the Protection of Birds, for example, now own and manage major tracts of land and draw on the support of hundreds of thousands of members. Britain is uniquely well served by these volunteers who set the standards for the rest of Europe and beyond.

Yet above all, it is the people who live in the countryside who have the most immediate interest in their local environment. Their local commitment, their time and enthusiasm and participation in voluntary schemes make the most important of contributions to improving the quality of their surroundings.

In all this, the Government has a rôle too. It must provide the legislative and policy framework within which the market operates and it must intervene where an unconstrained market fails to deliver the range of public benefits which we all expect of the countryside, urban or rural dweller alike. We must help land managers to achieve conservation goals by disseminating advice, information and training. Increasingly we must use incentives as a targeted and efficient mechanism to achieve public benefits in the countryside.

We must also use regulation as a necessary instrument with which to establish minimum standards, on matters like pollution and the use of pesticides. However, regulation is better at prohibiting certain practices than at encouraging initiative and cannot alone sustain sensitive management of the countryside. We therefore believe that regulation should be used sparingly and only when it is clearly necessary.

Often the best way to proceed is by national designations which protect areas of special environmental importance from the pressures of inappropriate development or intensive farming. But even here the touch must be as light as is consistent with effective protection.

Hedgerows

Hedgerows are distinctive features of the English countryside. They contribute positively to the character of the landscape and at the same time they provide shelter for crops and animals and help prevent soil erosion. Older hedgerows often contain a great diversity of plant and wildlife species and some can be of real historical interest.

So many hedgerows have been lost, through removal or more commonly neglect, that the Government has had to take action. We first asked the Countryside Commission to provide incentives to landowners to restore their hedgerows and manage them properly. Important hedges, such as ancient parish boundaries still remain vulnerable. We have therefore taken powers in the Environment Act 1995 to introduce regulations to protect them. **We will consult on these in draft with the aim of introducing them in the first half of 1996.**

The most effective protection for hedgerows, however, continues to lie in the hands of those who look after the land. They have a responsibility to manage hedgerows positively and to seek to protect and enhance their value.

Priority Areas

Since the Second World War our conservation efforts have responded to threats to landscape and wildlife by concentrating on the protection of the most important areas and sites. National Parks, for example, protect the most attractive landscapes, and Heritage Coasts the finest coastline. Sites of Special Scientific Interest conserve important wildlife habitats, while Special Protection Areas implement European legislation by protecting sites which are internationally important for birds and Special Areas of Conservation will, in future, protect areas of European importance for plants and animals.

Site of Special Scientific Interest, Frensham

Designations such as these help to conserve features which might otherwise have been lost. However, designating special areas is not, on its own, an adequate mechanism for conserving the quality of landscape and the abundance of wildlife which we all want to see. We can no longer afford to view designated areas in isolation from the rest of the countryside.

While it is important not to weaken protection of designated areas, the approaches pioneered in them can now be applied throughout our countryside. In order to complement the protection which designations offer to the special parts of our countryside, we need to build on the achievements of the past 50 years by finding new ways to enrich the quality of the wider countryside.

The Countryside Commission and English Nature are therefore working together on a common assessment of the distinctive features of our countryside in both landscape and nature conservation terms. This will lead to the production of a character map of the English countryside. The Government will ask the two agencies to report on their work by the end of 1995. We intend to:

- promote the work of this joint analysis;

- support the development and promotion of the project so that it can act as a focus for action to strengthen the distinctive character of the land and the built environment, not by encouraging new designations but as a means of extending the value of those we already have.

Countryside Character

By linking their existing Countryside Character programme and Natural Areas initiative, the Countryside Commission and English Nature will, for the first time, provide the comprehensive and consistent analysis of the character of the English countryside which our conservation efforts have hitherto lacked. The results of this joint project will help to guide all our efforts to conserve and enhance the countryside.

Whether we live in an urban or rural environment, our everyday enjoyment of the countryside depends most on areas closest to where we live. While these may not be of outstanding value in conservation or landscape terms, they have the greatest potential to meet our immediate needs for countryside recreation, not least because they minimise the need to travel. There is much that can be done to enhance them. For example, the Community Forest programme aims to improve the quality of the urban fringe so that more of us can enjoy the countryside close to home.

Forest of Mercia Team

Forest of Mercia Women's Institute at Pipe Hall

The Forest of Mercia

One of 12 Community Forest projects , the Forest of Mercia near Birmingham hopes to attract up to 20 million visitors a year by the time it is complete. European and urban regeneration grants have the potential to accelerate Community Forest programmes, and the Forest of Mercia has led the way with a successful bid for £238,000 from the European Regional Development Fund. This money has been used for an innovative strategy aimed at economic development and landscape enhancement.

The Forest's management team has worked in partnership with landowners and local authorities to improve over 150 hectares of land and acquire a 44 hectare farm for the creation of a new community woodland. A special unit is helping landowners to develop public access routes, and "Charcoal Enterprise" has been established with local businesses as part of a wider strategy to develop local markets for timber products.

Since the Second World War, Green Belts have helped to safeguard our countryside from urban encroachment and have been a considerable achievement of planning policy. They have been widely admired internationally. The fundamental aim of Green Belts is to prevent urban sprawl by keeping land permanently open. The use of land in Green Belts has a positive rôle to play in encouraging provision for outdoor sport and recreation as well as access to the countryside and in meeting other environmental and agricultural objectives.

It is the interdependence of town and country which needs to be stressed. A better environment in our towns and cities not only enhances the quality of life for those of us who live there but also helps to relieve pressure on the countryside. As a recent conference by the Council for the Protection of Rural England stressed, improving the urban environment is a prerequisite for the proper protection of rural England.

Several organisations already carry out valuable work in this field, including English Partnerships, the Countryside Commission, the Groundwork Trusts and English Nature. Local authorities and the private and voluntary sectors are also closely involved. **We will draw on the expertise of these bodies in order to develop national good practice for urban greening. This will aim to enhance the quality, design, conservation value and community use of open green space in order to make our towns and cities more attractive places in which to live.** It will look at ways in which we can capitalise on existing features, such as urban parks, road, rail and water corridors, street trees and playing fields, as well as the Community Forest projects. **We intend to initiate a public debate and publish a document by the end of 1996.**

The evolution of conservation policies has resulted in an overlapping network of designations, each of which has a particular focus and independent statutory basis and imposes a unique set of legal obligations. This can seem complex to landowners, occupiers and other interests. Whilst it would be difficult to remove or combine any of these designations, and we still have to honour some outstanding legal commitments, we believe that the current structure of types of designation is reasonably comprehensive. In order to further our objectives for sustainable land management our priority now should be to enhance the wider countryside. **The Government will therefore not introduce further classes of statutory designations.**

Over the years local authorities have introduced a multiplicity of local countryside designations. These may unduly discourage development without identifying the particular characteristics of the local countryside which need to be respected or enhanced.

We believe that more emphasis should be placed on identifying distinctive local characteristics and that authorities should only apply local countryside designations where normal planning policies cannot provide the necessary protection. **Our proposed revision of Planning Policy Guidance note 7, described in Chapter Two, will provide further advice to local planning authorities on this approach in the light of the emerging countryside character map.** This revision will not affect local nature conservation designations, which recognise the value of sites for wildlife.

Andrew Brown/Ecoscene

Hound Tor with Haytor and Haytor Rocks on horizon

National Parks

The seven National Parks in England, together with the Broads Authority, account for some 7.4% of the land area. They include many of England's finest landscapes and offer a wide range of opportunities to walk, ride, climb and undertake other outdoor pursuits.

The Environment Act 1995 reaffirms our continuing commitment to conserving and enhancing these areas and provides for the establishment of new, free-standing authorities to protect and manage them. The Act expands and brings up to date the Parks' conservation objectives and clarifies the enjoyment for which they are promoted. For the first time it places a duty on all public bodies to have regard to National Park purposes when carrying out their activities in them.

While it is recognised that conflicts could arise between the Parks' conservation and recreational purposes, it should prove possible to resolve the majority of them through management. Where irreconcilable conflict does occur, the Act states that the conservation purpose must prevail.

England's National Parks are not wildernesses. They are living, working landscapes where man's influence has shaped the very qualities for which they are valued. The 1995 Act emphasises the need for strong, positive relationships between the National Park authorities and those who live and work in the Parks. It enhances local representation in the authorities by the inclusion of members directly drawn from parish councils, strengthens liaison with local communities and places a duty on Park authorities to take the economic and social needs of those communities into account.

AGRICULTURE

Farming is central to the way in which the countryside is managed and is exceptional among industries in being so closely bound up with the management of the countryside environment. It occupies 76% of the land surface of England and has created the legacy of countryside features which the public values, including its hedgerows, meadow land and stone walls.

Chapter Two described the changing structure of agriculture, its significance as an employer and its part in the diversification of rural economic activity. What follows is a closer look at how farmers can integrate their production and marketing activities with stewardship of the countryside.

Farming's primary rôle is to produce food, a basic fact of life which is unlikely to change. In an age of plentiful food supplies, however, when shortage has given way to surplus, the environmental consequences of agricultural production have assumed growing importance for both consumers and policymakers.

Landscape and wildlife have been under pressure for decades. Countryside Survey recorded a decline in landscape features and the diversity of plant species in the general countryside, especially in the lowlands, while recent British Trust for Ornithology surveys show a marked decline in the populations of most farmland birds. Modern farming methods and techniques have been a major cause of these declines, although other factors, such as road building and development, have also made a substantial contribution.

In more recent years our policies, both nationally and through the Common Agricultural Policy, have been adjusted to give a much higher priority to environmental concerns. Where appropriate, regulation has been tightened up and a variety of incentive schemes, targeted at specific environmental objectives, has been introduced. Farmers themselves are keen to do more. We intend to build on the new awareness which exists of the need for positive action in order to sustain the beauty and diversity of the countryside and to reverse England's loss of wildlife and habitats. This opens up exciting prospects for the years ahead.

By providing improved information and advice and by making incentive schemes more widely available, we will encourage farmers wherever possible to work voluntarily towards these objectives.

The Red Kite Project

This project is a fine example of action to reverse the decline in our wildlife species. The Red Kite Project Team was established in 1986 to help reintroduce the Red Kite to this country. The Team comprised members from the Joint Nature Conservancy Council, English Nature, the Countryside Council for Wales, Scottish Natural Heritage, the Royal Society for the Protection of Birds and the Institute of Terrestrial Ecology.

Some 176 Red Kites have been secretly released in Britain and survival rates have been very good, with over 40% reaching breeding age in the north of Britain and 60% in the south. We hope that this action will result in a self-sustaining population of this impressive bird, which has not been seen in England since 1870.

Nest with chick

Incentive Schemes

Financial incentives are an important way of encouraging farmers and others to provide environmental benefits. They can be used to secure environmentally beneficial management which goes beyond normal responsible husbandry practices and the legal requirements placed on land managers.

Although it is not their primary purpose, incentive schemes can also help to create new jobs in the countryside, both directly by encouraging farmers to undertake works such as hedge laying or dry stone wall repair, and indirectly by sustaining the landscape and wildlife in ways which sustain rural tourism.

Traditional stone wall in the Peak District

Environmental Job Creation

In the Peak National Park a combination of advice and national and local incentive schemes has generated about 50 full time jobs in one year. Local contractors are carrying out work such as repairing walls, planting and maintaining hedges and shrubs, and creating new habitats.

Shropshire Hills Environmentally Sensitive Area

Through our environmental land management schemes, we give priority to areas, features and resources that:

● are valuable to the countryside but are in decline or under threat;

● have significant potential to provide new environmental benefits;

● are in need of positive management to maintain and enhance their value.

Over the last ten years or more, the Government and its agencies have developed a range of environmental land management schemes for the English countryside. In April 1984, we launched the Broads Grazing Marshes Conservation Scheme, the precursor for the Environmentally Sensitive Areas, which now cover some 1.1 million hectares of England, 10% of agricultural land, in 22 areas such as the Somerset Levels, the Shropshire Hills and the South Downs. Their purpose is to encourage environmentally beneficial farming techniques in large areas of the countryside noted for their natural beauty, rich habitats and historic interest.

New hedge in Hereford and Worcester funded by the Countryside Stewardship Scheme

In 1991 the Countryside Commission launched Countryside Stewardship as a five year pilot project to test whether a system of discretionary payments, potentially available throughout England, could achieve a broad range of environmental objectives through a single integrated scheme. This pilot scheme has been a success. The completion of Countryside Stewardship's pilot phase in April 1996, and the transfer of the scheme to the Ministry of Agriculture, Fisheries and Food (MAFF), will represent a landmark in the development of environmental land management schemes.

A range of new incentive schemes to encourage environmentally friendly farming has followed in rapid order since the beginning of 1994. These initiatives were developed under the European agri-environment regulation which was an important element in the 1992 reform of the CAP, and one which the United Kingdom played a major part in securing.

Recent Incentive Schemes:

- a Habitat Scheme to create or improve a range of habitats over a 20 year period;

- a Moorland Scheme to protect and improve the condition of heather and other shrubby moorland;

- 22 new Nitrate Sensitive Areas to protect selected groundwater sources used to supply drinking water;

- an Organic Aid Scheme to encourage conversion to organic production methods;

- a Countryside Access Scheme to increase opportunities for public access to set-aside land;

- new payments to increase opportunities for public access to the countryside within Environmentally Sensitive Areas.

Countryside Access Scheme
Signboard and way marker,
Boxworth Research Centre

The number of schemes in place at present reflects the great diversity of the English countryside and the range of the our environmental objectives, covering landscape, habitats, wildlife, natural resources, archaeological and historic features and public access. However, following the growth in the number of schemes in recent years, we reviewed the future rôle of Stewardship and the integration and focus of all the environmental land management schemes and consulted in the spring of 1995 on the recommendations of a working group.

In the light of the endorsement of the broad thrust of the proposals, we have now decided on our next steps. Regarding Countryside Stewardship we will:

- give high priority to providing the extra funds necessary to enable Stewardship to continue to grow as the Government's main incentive scheme for the wider countryside outside Environmentally Sensitive Areas;

- retain the key features of the pilot scheme, including its flexibility and use of discretion and targeting to achieve best value for money;

- retain the full range of existing options within Stewardship, and add two new options targeting traditional stone walls and banks and the remaining unimproved areas of old meadow and pasture on neutral and acid soils throughout lowland England;

- further expand Stewardship by integrating with it payments for conservation purposes under the Farm and Conservation Grants Scheme; and consider further the integration with Stewardship of the Habitat Scheme, the Countryside Access Scheme and the Moorland Scheme when they complete their pilot phase in 1998/99.

As schemes grow it is important to make sure that they remain targeted on the benefits they are intended to achieve and that they complement each other effectively. **In order to keep under review the integration and focus of environmental land management schemes, MAFF will establish a steering group involving the Department of the Environment, the Countryside Commission, English Heritage and English Nature to advise on:**

- the objectives, targets and priorities of environmental land management schemes;

- their development, deployment, monitoring and evaluation;

- their rôle alongside other regulatory and advisory mechanisms for enhancing the environment.

We will also create a new national forum for regular consultation with a wide variety of interested parties to inform our thinking.

It is important for incentive schemes to be responsive to local and regional character. We will put in place arrangements in each region for consultation on the operation of these environmental schemes. At a local level we will consider how to harness the expertise of local organisations to get the best value out of the schemes.

Common Land

The 350,000 hectares of common land in England remain important for farmers in the uplands, as well as being a major ecological resource and opportunity for open air recreation. We remain committed to maintaining the status of common land, to protecting the rights of commoners and to encouraging proper management. In 1996 we will commission a management guide to identify and publicise best practice in managing common land.

There are deficiencies in the legislative framework governing commons. In particular, the present rules on registration have created anomalies, and there is concern that management arrangements do not allow for common land to participate fully in the schemes now available to promote environmentally friendly agriculture. We do not now believe that comprehensive legislation, along the lines of that proposed in 1986 by the Common Land Forum, is feasible or practical. However, in order to improve matters we will:

- support solutions tailored to local circumstances, as proposed in relation to Dartmoor and Bodmin Moor;

- work with those who use and manage common land to identify practical solutions to the worst registration and management problems, and consult widely on measures to remedy these.

Advice and Information

Farmers' efforts to maintain and improve the environment can benefit substantially from sound advice and encouragement, especially where it reinforces regulation or incentives. With this in mind the Government has published three Codes of Good Agricultural Practice. Together these form a body of practical advice on how to farm in a way which protects and enhances the quality of water, air and soil. The Codes are based on the best available scientific knowledge, and are updated to keep pace with current knowledge and concerns. With the help of market research, we are reviewing the Codes in order to ensure that they are accessible and easy to understand. Our aim is to improve farmers' awareness of the Codes and their uptake of the advice in them. We will keep the effectiveness of the Codes under review.

Face-to-face advice is also available to farmers through free pollution visits and farm waste management plans provided by ADAS. The Government funds some 3,000 farm pollution visits and 1,300 free conservation advice visits by ADAS each year.

The Farming and Wildlife Advisory Group (FWAG) also provides on-farm conservation advice and is successfully encouraging farmers to develop whole farm plans as a way of helping them identify ways of conserving and enhancing wildlife habitats, while at the same time maintaining profitable farming. FWAG has recently reviewed its future strategy and we look forward to working with FWAG to improve the extent and effectiveness of its conservation advice.

Farming and Wildlife Advisory Group providing training to staff from Booker at Elton, Cambridgeshire

The development and encouragement of lower input farming systems is attracting a great deal of attention. Government and industry are funding a range of research projects to investigate ways of reducing the reliance of arable production on inputs such as pesticides and bought-in fertilisers. The Integrated Arable Crop Production Alliance has been formed to bring together a number of groups working in this field in order to improve coordination and to ensure the effective dissemination of the research results.

A particular area of activity concerns pesticides. Despite their economic advantages many pesticides are potentially harmful to wildlife. Research has shown that their use has contributed to the decline of certain farmland bird species by, for example, reducing their insect feedstock.

Our policy is to limit pesticide use to the minimum necessary for effective pest control, subject to overriding considerations of human health and environmental impact. We restrict the pesticides which are available to farmers through an approvals procedure and also control, by regulations, the ways in which approved pesticides may be applied. Farmers and growers themselves can reduce pesticide usage by improving their methods and procedures; and retailers and their customers could contribute if they were prepared to accept, for example, fruit and vegetables with a small amount of pest damage. **In order to further our policy on the use of pesticides we will hold a conference in October 1995 to help us develop an Action Plan. In addition, as part of a wider exercise, we are helping to review the pesticides in use throughout the European Union to ensure that they meet high safety standards.**

Action Plan for Responsible Use of Pesticides

Features of the Action Plan are likely to include:

• working with farmers, growers, retailers, consumers and other organisations to encourage widespread adoption of pesticide minimisation techniques;

• promoting these techniques through formal and ad hoc training, guidance and the extension services;

• investigating and promoting the opportunities afforded by new technology and research;

• reporting progress annually to the Advisory Committee on Pesticides.

Moorley Research Centre

Experiments at Morley Research Centre in Norfolk are using targeted fungicide programmes on select varieties of cereals. Results show that considerable savings in the costs and amounts of pesticide use can be achieved with no loss of crop yield or quality

There is much which farmers and their customers, particularly retailers, can do to minimise any adverse environmental impact of farming. Crop rotations, the use of pest and disease resistant varieties, matching crops to soil type and climate, the provision of habitats for pest predators, the proper assessment of crop nutrient requirements and the precision use of machinery in applying pesticides and fertilisers can all make a substantial contribution. The careful use of such established husbandry practices and procedures is often referred to as Integrated Crop Management. We want to see such techniques adopted more widely.

In this connection, MAFF is undertaking research, in conjunction with industry, under the LINK programme 'Technologies for Sustainable Farming', which has as one of its main priorities the development of novel methods of pest, disease and weed control. As an example, one project is aimed at developing non-lethal sprays to prevent slug damage to crops. The sprays, using compounds produced naturally by certain plants as a deterrent mechanism against slugs and snails, would replace the use of poisonous molluscicides.

We welcome initiatives by groups such as LEAF (Linking Environment and Farming), the National Farmers' Union (NFU) and retailers to encourage integrated crop management and similar farming practices. LEAF's Environmental Audit provides a valuable checklist for farmers wishing to review their operations. The NFU has agreed production protocols for most horticultural crops with a group of multiple retailers which are aimed particularly at limiting pesticide use to the minimum necessary. There is scope too for producers and other interests to identify market opportunities for distinctive products, part of whose attraction lies in the fact that their production is environmentally friendly.

Louise Rawling/Herdwick Sheep Association

Herdwick sheep with shepherd at Ulpha in the Duddon Valley

Herdwick Carpets

Herdwick sheep are the traditional breed which graze extensively in the Lake District, and they are well suited to managing the unimproved upland grasslands. Their wool, however, is wiry and unsuitable for most clothing. In order to help maintain the economic viability of the breed, the National Trust has worked with Gaskell Carpets in Skipton to develop and market naturally tinted Herdwick carpets, emphasising the rôle of the flocks in sustaining the traditional landscape of the Lake District.

Traditional Apple Orchards

In Somerset, Pass Vale Farm is maintaining the commercial viability of 50 acres of traditional apple orchards by diversifying the end product away from the more commonplace cider towards the production of cider brandy. The initiative adds extra value to the crop and is designed to ensure a profitable outlet for traditional cider apple growers.

Organic farming is one area where the market is able to play a part in encouraging more environmentally friendly farming, and we are encouraging farmers to respond to those market signals. Organic farmers receive the same support from the Common Agricultural Policy (CAP) as conventional farmers but generally experience lower yields and require a fertility building phase in their rotations. Recent reforms to the CAP, described below, have benefited organic farmers and many will qualify for environmental incentive payments such as those under Countryside Stewardship, Environmentally Sensitive Areas and Nitrate Sensitive Areas agreements, as well as under the Organic Aid Scheme. We intend to do more to make existing and potential organic farmers aware of these developments. In addition, statutory organic production standards and regular inspections protect producers and consumers from fraud. We also fund an extensive programme of research with an annual budget of £1 million, and provide support for the United Kingdom Register of Organic Food Standards.

The Common Agricultural Policy

It is not possible to assess precisely the extent to which the CAP, or the United Kingdom's deficiency payments system before it, have contributed to the adverse environmental consequences of some aspects of modern farming. Both have certainly caused some adverse effects, largely through high support prices which have, for example, encouraged the ploughing up of grassland for cereals cultivation. More generally, high support prices have stimulated the adoption of more intensive farming methods, such as the greater use of pesticides and fertilisers.

In more recent years changes to the CAP have taken increasing account of the need to safeguard the environment. Greening the CAP has been a consistent UK objective in the Council of Agriculture Ministers for a number of years. A change to the rules so that conditions to discourage overgrazing could be attached to livestock payments was a notable success. In the absence of appropriate conditions, payments dependent on the number of animals on a farm can encourage overstocking and overgrazing, a matter of particular concern in sensitive upland areas. Conditions and potential penalties now apply to all the premium schemes operating in the United Kingdom, and we intend to keep their effectiveness under close review.

Cross-compliance, which involves attaching environmental conditions to CAP payments, aims to ensure that support payments do not promote environmental damage but are consistent with the objectives of the agri-environmental incentive schemes. To date the most extensive application of cross-compliance has been on set-aside land, where farmers are required to comply with a list of environmental conditions in order to qualify for payment. In this particular case the application of cross-compliance is an obligation binding on all European Member States. We are committed to looking for ways of extending cross-compliance wherever it is practicable and sensible to do so.

Cross-Compliance

The Department of the Environment and the Dutch Ministry of Agriculture, Nature Management and Fisheries have jointly commissioned a study[1] to examine the scope for wider application of cross-compliance conditions. The report, by the Institute of European Environmental Policy, considers examples of cross-compliance from within the European Union and beyond and discusses policy options for extending its rôle. We shall publish the report in October 1995 and disseminate it with a view to stimulating informed debate across Europe.

In June 1995, we achieved a further important objective when the Council of Ministers agreed that in future arable land taken out of production under agri-environment schemes, currently the Nitrate Sensitive Areas and Habitat Schemes, and forestry schemes could count against farmers' set-aside obligations. This should encourage farmers to participate in those schemes. We will continue to look for new ways of maximising the potential environmental benefits of set-aside. MAFF has commissioned a three year evaluation of set-aside by the Institute of Terrestrial Ecology, the British Trust for Ornithology and ADAS. They will recommend changes to the present management rules in order to maximise the benefits to wildlife.

Further Reform of the CAP

Chapter Two set out our objectives for reform of the CAP, including a much greater emphasis on safeguarding and enhancing the rural environment. If put into practice, these changes would remove a large part of the apparatus of quotas, income support and bureaucratic regulation which at present exists under the CAP.

The Minister of Agriculture's CAP Review Group, whose conclusions were published in July 1995, recognised that reducing support should relieve pressure for intensive use of land but considered that there might also be reduced positive management of environmental features. In the absence of complementary measures, the Review Group anticipated that reform would lead to a mixture of positive and negative outcomes for the environment. Reductions in production-related support should not be seen as a panacea for the environment. Likely positive effects would include:

- a drop in overall use of agrochemical inputs;

- a reversion of some former grassland now in arable use to extensive livestock grazing.

Likely negative effects would include:

- a boost for intensive livestock farming at the expense of extensive grazing, because of lower cereals prices;

- a reduction in voluntary management of environmental features such as hedges, stone walls and woodlands, because of a drop in farm incomes and the farm labour force.

---

[1] *Cross-compliance Within the Common Agricultural Policy: a review of options for landscape and nature conservation; Institute for European Environmental Policy, 1995, HMSO*

It is probable therefore that there will be a continuing and perhaps increasing need for incentive schemes with specific environmental objectives. We would like to see a part of the savings from the reductions in production-oriented support made available for this purpose. We will continue to make every effort to ensure that care for the environment is central to the development of the CAP in the years to come.

The future of the Common Agricultural Policy is a matter for the whole of the European Union to decide upon. We will seek support for our CAP objectives so as to ensure that sensible and rational policies prevail. The European Commission has an important rôle to play because it - not the Member States - has the right formally to propose changes to European legislation. We will press for the closer integration of environmental and agricultural policymaking within the Commission, for example through the inclusion of environmental and consumer representatives on the Commission's agricultural advisory committees.

Ministry of Defence Land

The Ministry of Defence (MOD) manages about 476,000 acres of land in England, mostly for training in rural areas where its presence can bring considerable economic and social benefits. Because many training areas have been protected from intensive farming and development they contain some of our most important sites for landscape, archaeology and nature conservation. MOD recognises its responsibilities to conserve these important areas and will:

Tawny Owl nesting in an ammunition box

- continue to incorporate conservation objectives in its plans for the care and management of sites;

- aim to ensure that any new developments in the open countryside will be of high quality and will be sensitive to the local environment;

- ensure that troops taking part in training exercises are made fully aware of their responsibilities towards conservation in sensitive areas;

- continue to work closely with national conservation groups on the environmental management of the Defence Estate;

- continue to develop formal agreements with English Nature for the management of sensitive sites such as Sites of Special Scientific Interest and work jointly with Department of the Environment on policies for protecting sites designated under the Habitats and Birds Directives.

MOD will continue to give a high priority to conservation despite an inevitable increase in training as a result of withdrawal of troops from Germany. It will consult appropriate local and environmental interests, including the Countryside Commission, about proposals to intensify training significantly and where appropriate will carry out Environmental Impact Assessments. It will also develop new land management systems to protect the environment alongside proposals for increasing training. For example, new tracks are being laid on Salisbury Plain to prevent unacceptable damage from heavy vehicles and exercises may be halted in adverse weather conditions where they could lead to damage.

MOD will continue to encourage public access to the Defence Estate. It will publish a revised edition of the booklet _Walks on MOD Lands_ before the end of the year and is reviewing its policy on access with a view to enhancing access while recognising the need for public safety.

FORESTRY

Broadleaved woodland near Oakshott in the East Hampshire Area of Outstanding Natural Beauty

The planting of trees is a sign of our confidence in the future. It is a compliment paid by our generation to its successors and marks our gratitude to those who paid us that compliment in the past. From the majesty of a great avenue to the single specimen in a suburban garden, trees enhance our lives and lift our spirits. They shelter our wildlife and temper our climate. They provide resources and employment which is especially welcome in areas where the land produces little. Yet however we may celebrate them, the trees we enjoy today are but the living remnant of those that once grew all over England.

Many centuries ago, up to 80% of Britain was covered by forest. This was steadily cleared for farming and settlement until by 1000 A.D. forest cover had fallen to around 20%, and by the end of the First World War had reached a low of 5%. Since then, support for forestry has helped to increase woodland cover to around 10% in Britain as a whole, and to about 7% in England. Even so we have about the smallest area of woodland in Europe.

Farm woodland

Until recently this expansion was driven mainly by a desire to increase timber production in order to reduce our dependence on imports. But this sometimes caused environmental damage with poorly designed forest marring the landscape or taking insufficient account of the importance of the land for wildlife.

Much has been learned from this experience. We now understand how essential it is to ensure that landscape, wildlife, water, archaeological and recreational interests are taken fully into account. Forestry now offers new opportunities for recreation and leisure, for wildlife conservation and for enhancing the landscape. Both new planting and sound management of existing woodland have their part to play.

New Planting

England is more densely populated than most other European countries, and so forestry is in closer competition with other land uses. Unlike many of our neighbours, we remain heavily dependent on imported timber, with as much as 90% of the wood products we use coming from abroad. The forestry programmes of recent decades will double our timber production in the next twenty years. We are also providing for a steady expansion of broadleaved woodland so that four hectares of broadleaved trees are now planted for every one of conifers.

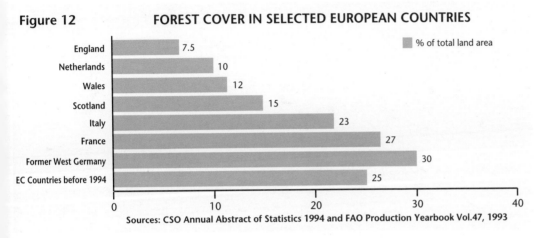

Figure 12   **FOREST COVER IN SELECTED EUROPEAN COUNTRIES**

Sources: CSO Annual Abstract of Statistics 1994 and FAO Production Yearbook Vol.47, 1993

The key to a major expansion of forestry lies in changes to the Common Agricultural Policy. If production related support for farming is progressively reduced, as we propose, forestry will be able to compete for land use on more equal terms with farming. These changes may be some years ahead, and even then there are still likely to be many circumstances where woodland will not be competitive. Nevertheless the Government would like to see a doubling of woodland in England over the next half century and believes that this will be possible given the range of incentives already in place and the necessary future changes in the Common Agricultural Policy.

A continued and significant expansion of woodland will bring many benefits. It will improve the appearance of the countryside, create new jobs, enrich wildlife habitats and open up new opportunities for recreation. It will even help to improve air quality in areas affected by traffic pollution and lead to a greater absorption of carbon dioxide.

Tree planting is likely to be most beneficial where it:

- enhances the landscape close to centres of population, because this is where people will most appreciate it;

- creates new recreational opportunities;

- makes a positive contribution to the quality of the countryside, for example by restoring degraded land;

- complements and expands existing woodland which is a part of the countryside's heritage.

The Government will work in close cooperation with local authorities, landowners, voluntary organisations and others in order to encourage such planting.

Community and National Forests

Community Forests

The joint initiative of the Countryside Commission and the Forestry Commission to develop Community Forests on the fringe of urban centres will bring important environmental benefits to these areas. Teams have been established to work in partnership with local interests. We have now approved detailed business plans for the development of all 12 Forests and are making higher rates of planting grant available on a localised basis in the Community Forest areas.

The National Forest

A new National Forest is to be created in the heart of England, linking what remains of the ancient forests of Needwood and Charnwood. Eventually about one third of the area will be wooded, providing an attractive setting for farmland, open country, towns and villages. The project will promote economic regeneration by improving the landscape of an area largely bereft of woodland and scarred by industrial activities of the past. It will create new recreational opportunities as well as new wildlife habitats.

The National Forest stemmed from the vision of the Countryside Commission which carried out the initial feasibility and preparatory work. In April 1995 the Government launched a new body to turn this vision into a reality. Jointly sponsored by the Department of the Environment and the Forestry Commission, the National Forest Company will work in partnership with Ministry of Agriculture, Fisheries and Food, local authorities, voluntary groups, mineral and other commercial companies as well as with local farmers and landowners.

Targeting of Grants

As of 1995, for the first time, higher rates of grant are available in priority areas. In the National Forest, we are piloting a new approach to forestry grants by inviting landowners to put forward competitive tenders for up to £1 million of grants additional to those offered under the Forestry Commission's Woodland Grant Scheme. Tenders must specify the economic, environmental and amenity benefits which their projects will provide. The National Forest Company will support those projects which contribute most towards the development of the forest and which offer the greatest value for money. It will announce the winners of the first year's competition in the autumn of 1995. In parts of the Community Forests, we are offering a flat rate locational supplement of £600 per hectare in addition to normal grant payments. If these schemes are successful we will consider extending these approaches to other areas.

Environmental Regeneration

Forestry has the potential to transform derelict and degraded land. It is unacceptable that land should remain an eyesore especially in a densely populated country such as ours. We therefore seek to find new ways of using forestry techniques in the service of environmental regeneration. The following examples illustrate how we intend to proceed:

- the National Urban Forestry Unit, which was launched in July 1995, will demonstrate how innovative and cost effective planting techniques can create attractive landscapes in urban areas and on degraded land. The Unit will work in close partnership with the Groundwork Foundation and the network of Groundwork Trusts as well as other bodies such as English Partnerships, the Countryside Commission and the Forestry Authority;

- English Partnerships, the Government's main agency for land regeneration, is committed to using modern forestry techniques imaginatively to restore derelict land, to promote greening of urban areas and to provide attractive settings for redevelopment. It will work with the National Forest, the Community Forests, the Forestry Commission and the new Urban Forestry Unit on regional strategies for forestry. It will also work closely with Groundwork on community led environmental improvement projects;

- the new Government Offices for the Regions, described in Chapter Two, administer regionally Government and European regeneration programmes. Forestry has the potential to take a much greater part in these programmes and to contribute to the integration of environmental and economic objectives. The Forestry Commission will therefore develop closer working links with the Government Offices to achieve this end.

Farm Woodland

Planting trees is one way in which farmers can diversify their activity while adding variety to the landscape of lowland areas. Since farm woodland schemes were first introduced in 1988, some 20 million trees have been planted on farms in England - most of them broadleaved. The changes which we have secured to European rules on the use of set-aside land, described in the Agriculture section of this Chapter, should give a further boost to on-farm woodland planting. Allowing land planted under forestry schemes to count as set aside is fully consistent with European policies to integrate environmental concerns with the achievement of other social and economic goals.

Woodland Management

Good management of woodland brings both economic and environmental benefits. Yet many broadleaved woodlands are not well managed. Over the last ten years, the Forestry Commission and other bodies have funded a number of small scale woodland projects which have sought to improve the management and utilisation of neglected woodlands. Some of the projects have promoted the marketing of hardwood products as a way of adding value to the woodlands and encouraging better management. The Forestry Commission and the Department of the Environment have commissioned a joint study into these projects in order to identify best practice and to promote it more widely.

Tarn Hows near Coniston, Lake District National Park, with forestry sympathetic to landscape

Andrew Brown/Ecoscene

Drawing on the results of this joint study, the Forestry Commission will undertake a new programme to promote good woodland management. It will provide advice and training to owners on how to realise the economic potential of their woodlands, promote better links between owners, contractors and customers and advise on the development of new products and markets for hardwood.

The East Anglian Woodlands Project

This project aims to assist over 10,000 woodland owners to bring neglected woodlands into management. The project has been successful in developing new markets, such as charcoal, brushwood for river-bank reinforcement and canal piling using alder. It is now beginning to make inroads into an estimated £3 million market in East Anglia for firewood sold on petrol station forecourts. At present, most of this firewood is imported. The Forestry Authority is supporting the project in close partnership with the Countryside Commission and the Norfolk, Suffolk, Essex and Cambridgeshire County Councils.

Access

Unless there are good management reasons for preventing it, Forestry Commission woodlands allow public access for recreation. In recognition of the recreational value of these woodlands to the public the Government is reviewing ways of protecting access to them in the event of their sale to the private sector.

Private owners of woodland are actively encouraged to allow public access for recreational purposes. Following our review of forestry incentives in 1994 we have introduced a new discretionary Woodland Improvement Grant which will be targeted at access and recreation schemes in its first year. The Forestry Commission has reinforced this support by publishing guidelines for woodland owners on how to provide access and recreational opportunities.

Monitoring

In the summer of 1995, the Forestry Commission began work on a computerised inventory which will provide the most accurate picture ever of the size, structure and condition of England's woodlands. This detailed survey will assess the condition of woodlands as a wildlife conservation and recreation resource, forecast timber production for the wood processing industries and monitor forestry initiatives such as planting on farmland and the creation of Community Forests. The inventory will help us to base our forestry programmes on sound information and to measure their future success.

Walkers at Newlands Corner Reserve, North Downs

RECREATION AND ACCESS

Recreation

As Chapter Two explains, recreation is a particularly important source of income and employment in rural areas. Most visits are made close to home, half involving a round trip of less than five miles and walking remains by far our most popular pursuit. There are, however, many other increasing demands upon the countryside as a place for recreation. These have to be reconciled and no single interest ought to dominate to the exclusion of all others. Not least this is because the enjoyment of the countryside properly consists in appreciating its variety and the many different facets of rural life.

For example, recreation and wildlife co-exist well. Those who come to enjoy the countryside wish to see a high quality landscape rich in wildlife. Many areas which have been primarily created for recreational purposes, such as country parks, urban commons and National Trust open space, have become important wildlife sites too.

Large numbers of visitors, and the traffic they generate, can put pressure on the environment of some of the most attractive parts of England's countryside, not least our National Parks. But as the Environment Select Committee acknowledged in the summer of 1995, the evidence suggests that the adverse impact of leisure activities is often exaggerated, and good management can overcome most problems.

That positive management can also help prevent conflict. Anglers and canoeists, walkers and field sport enthusiasts, visitors and local communities need to find ways of accommodating each other's activities.

Policies need to reflect these considerations, and our priorities are therefore to:

- promote countryside recreation because it enriches the nation as a whole;

- pursue policies which enable people to enjoy the countryside close to where they live;

- seek to ensure that countryside recreation takes place in ways which cause no lasting damage to the environment and respects other rural interests;

- encourage creative management of recreation in order to anticipate conflicts and resolve them at an early stage.

The Countryside Commission promotes and manages countryside recreation. But recreation must not be seen in isolation. Sport and tourism are important too and, in order to achieve proper integration of these activities, we need to assess their environmental impact and their contribution to the economy and well-being of rural communities. **We will therefore ask the Countryside Commission to develop collaborative programmes with the Rural Development Commission, the Sports Council and the English Tourist Board to meet this objective.**

Those who live in the countryside often have surprisingly limited access to sports facilities, and although they may be surrounded by open space, this is not necessarily space which they can use. The Government recognises their particular needs and will look for ways of making better use of playing fields and other facilities attached to schools or other public institutions. The Sports Council will consider applications for National Lottery funding from local authorities and others in support of projects designed to enhance countryside recreation.

Leisure activities have diversified in recent years, with an increasing demand for activities such as golf, hang gliding and mountain biking. Other increasingly popular activities, such as clay pigeon shooting and motor sports, can cause disturbance to residents and visitors. Our objective is to enable a wide range of pursuits to be enjoyed in ways which minimise noise and disturbance to others. We seek to ensure that an appropriate balance is struck both through the planning system and by encouraging codes of practice.

Planning Policy Guidance note 17, *Sport and Recreation*, advises local planning authorities on providing for the sport and recreation needs of residents and visitors in the countryside. **We will commission research into its effectiveness, and will examine the implications for the countryside and planning of rapidly growing leisure activities, including noisy and obtrusive activities.**

However, this must not all be one way. We must become more determined to fulfil our obligations than to insist upon our rights. Visitors have responsibilities towards the countryside and towards those who live in it and own and care for it.

We will therefore ask the Countryside Commission to review ways of increasing public awareness of the responsibilities we all have, so that we can better foster understanding between urban and rural England.

Access to the Countryside

It is in this spirit that we can best approach the issue of access. Access is essential to our enjoyment of the countryside and we are committed to improving public access for all, be they walkers, riders or cyclists. We have special concern for people with disabilities. As a long term goal, we would like to see everyone, whether they live in town or country, have access to quality green space within a reasonable distance from their homes.

The Wyre Estuary Country Park

At this country park in Lancashire, Wyre Borough Council has provided a range of facilities in response to a demand for countryside recreation from local disabled people, who are now actively encouraged to visit the park. Facilities include the Wyreside Trail, a circular walk with a tapping rail and audio tape suitable for people with visual impairment and also a birdhide which has low level viewing for wheelchair users. The Wyreside Ecology Centre within the Park contains tactile exhibits, accessible toilets and room to manoeuvre wheelchairs.

Wyre Borough Council

The Council won the first national award of the BT Countryside for All project which aims to make the countryside more accessible for people with disabilities.

In some parts of the countryside, freedom to roam is appropriate. For example the Forestry Commission allows walkers unrestricted access to most of its land, except where this would be dangerous. However, we believe that a general right to roam, conflicting with other uses of land, leading to damage to crops or causing danger to livestock or disturbance of wildlife, and denying the rights of landowners, is not acceptable. It would elevate one interest above all others and institutionalise rights without obligations.

Already the rights of way network provides 120,000 miles of footpaths and bridleways for all of us to enjoy. Despite some shortcomings, it offers the best means of securing public access in a manner which respects the rights and interests of local people, farmers and landowners.

A valuable legacy from an earlier age, the network has not always been properly maintained or well publicised. In addition, the definitive maps on which public rights of way should be recorded, and which provide the legal framework for positive management of access, are still incomplete. These deficiencies need to be remedied, and in the 1990 Environment White Paper, *This Common Inheritance*, the Government adopted the target of bringing the network into good order by the year 2000.

Much work is needed if this target is to be reached. The main responsibility for protecting and maintaining rights of way lies with the highways authorities, some 82% of which have adopted the target and are giving rights of way high priority. This is reflected in the significant additional resources which they have begun to devote to this task.

As a result, a Countryside Commission survey carried out in 1994 revealed a significant improvement in the condition of the rights of way network. However, much work remains to be done. In 1993, the Commission introduced the Milestones initiative to encourage authorities to draw up clear action plans. Milestones Statements involve establishing what has already been achieved and what remains to be done, determining priorities and a timetable for action and allocating the resources which are necessary to achieve the target. From April 1996, the Commission will only consider offering grant to authorities which have identified clear needs and priorities in a Milestones Statement or similar strategic document.

Footpaths, bridleways, byways and rural roads often reflect earlier patterns of travel, whether to work, to church or between parishes. This is part of their fascination today. However a very different network might emerge if it were planned with the needs of today's walkers, riders, or cyclists in mind, and the existing pattern of rights of way sometimes fails to meet the expectations of local people and the general public alike.

Many see the present procedures for changing rights of way as cumbersome. It has, for example, proved difficult to progress packages of proposals designed to meet the needs of an area, such as a parish, and which are more satisfactory for both walkers and land managers.

The proper maintenance of rights of way and the effective management of their use are both necessary in order to provide the access that so many of us want in ways which do not conflict with the needs of those who live and work in the countryside. Local people share a responsibility for managing their environment, especially since they are often best placed to identify what needs to be done and to take appropriate action. The rights of way network offers particular scope for local action.

Parish Paths

The Countryside Commission's Parish Paths Partnership initiative, launched in 1992, offers grants to parish councils to encourage them to manage local footpaths and bridleways. By March 1995, over 900 parishes were participating in the scheme, which is having a marked impact and has improved relations between landowners and local volunteers. We commend the effectiveness of the Parish Paths Partnership initiative, but also wish to identify further ways of encouraging direct management at the local level.

Parish councils already have some powers to require highway authorities to take action on rights of way. They can also negotiate with the highway authority to take on maintenance of footpaths and bridleways within their area. In practice very few exercise this power, and authorities are sometimes reluctant to delegate functions. We will therefore stimulate the more active participation of parish councils in footpath management by encouraging three or four parish councils to group together to make the task more practicable. The Government will test this approach by inviting the Countryside Commission to cooperate with it in developing a pilot project to build on the experience of the Parish Paths Partnership.

In evaluating this project, we will consider whether there are ways of making the system for changing rights of way simpler and more flexible, and we will consult on proposals. A fundamental principle will continue to be that any change should not lead to a net loss of access, but should improve the overall quality of public access to the countryside.

Vehicles on Byways

While the greater part of the rights of way network is devoted exclusively to the needs of walkers, riders and cyclists, conflicts can occur in relation to the 4% which can be used by motorised vehicles. Traditionally, these byways were used largely by agricultural vehicles, but in recent decades there has been a growth in their use by 4-wheel drive and other vehicles for recreational purposes. Many people have expressed concern about the damage and disturbance which the inconsiderate use of such vehicles can cause, and about the illegal use by vehicles of footpaths, bridleways and open land.

Although damage can be severe where it occurs and is exacerbated by bad weather, the problem is limited to a tiny proportion of the network. However, in recognition of public concerns, we will:

- encourage highways authorities to use their existing powers, including the making of Traffic Regulation Orders, to control or prohibit vehicular use;

- encourage authorities to promote responsible use and practical conservation and maintenance work;

- review the most effective ways of managing vehicles' use of rights of way and prepare better advice to highways authorities on best practice.

It has been suggested that the Government should introduce general legislation to protect byways, by banning motorised vehicles from them except for access to property. We do not believe that a conclusive case has been made for such action. Nevertheless, we will discuss this issue further with the Local Authority Associations and others with an interest, to see whether general legislation may be desirable.

River Corridors

Rivers are one of our most underused assets. They have great potential to provide attractive walks along their banks and to link town with country. We will therefore invite the Countryside Commission and the National Rivers Authority to explore ways of focusing those resources which are earmarked for river restoration, landscape enhancement and access improvements onto river corridors in the countryside around cities. Local people will be encouraged to take part in developing suitable schemes.

Inland Waterways

Developed originally for freight transport, England's waterways are a unique legacy. They are widely used for angling, walking and pleasure boating. They form a link between rural and urban areas which is rich in both wildlife and historic structures, and in addition they fulfil a valuable function in water supply, flood defence and land drainage.

Planning Policy Guidance note 13, *Transport*, encourages local planning authorities to include policies and proposals for developing the potential of inland waterways in their development plans, and the British Waterways Board is doing much to increase access. There is also a strong tradition of voluntary work which has seen volunteers take responsibility for many restoration and preservation projects, sometimes with the support of the Environmental Action Fund and English Partnerships' land reclamation programmes.

Kennet and Avon Canal Trust

Caen Hill flight, Devizes

The Kennet and Avon Canal

The Kennet and Avon Canal is a fine example of how local volunteers can take action to improve their environment. Completed in 1810, the canal prospered as a transport route until the arrival of the railway. It was closed to traffic in 1951, falling into total disrepair. In 1962 the newly formed Kennet and Avon Canal Trust began the largest civil engineering project ever undertaken by volunteers, completing its restoration in partnership with British Waterways and local authorities. The canal's 87 miles were formally reopened by Her Majesty The Queen in 1990. The Trust has a continuing rôle in improving and maintaining facilities, in particular maintaining the long term water supply for the canal and its unique flight of 29 locks at Devizes.

The National Rivers Authority and the British Waterways Board maintain and enhance waterways for leisure and commercial purposes and in order to safeguard heritage and habitats. In February 1995 we issued a consultation paper seeking views on the future administration of these waterways to help us decide how best to ensure their stewardship for the 21st century. We expect to publish our response to the consultation before the end of 1995.

DEVELOPMENT IN THE COUNTRYSIDE

We are now more acutely conscious than ever before of man's power to harm his environment. The planet is no longer seen as a place of inexhaustible riches and indestructible systems. The gigantic strides we have made in technology and science have given us the ability to destroy

Mike Williams/Countryside Commission

Bakewell, Peak District National Park

and also the means to recreate and restore. Increasingly we have become aware of the limits of scarce and non-renewable resources, and of the heavy demands that today's western lifestyles place on them. Although the countryside is more resilient than many have feared, it is still enormously vulnerable and the pressures upon it need to be managed with care.

Sustainable development challenges us all to accommodate development in ways which protect or enhance the environment. Painful experience of past mistakes has made development a pejorative word for many people in the countryside. This makes it all the more important to assess the impacts of development on the environment, particularly where resources are not renewable or where the effects may be irreversible, and to find ways of:

- managing demand for land and other valuable resources more prudently, for example by targeting as much new building as possible on land which has already been developed, rather than on green field sites;

- ensuring that natural resources are used in ways that minimise harm to the surrounding environment;

- designing necessary development with more imagination and sensitivity so that it reinforces local character and is acceptable to local people.

Coastal Management

The need to reconcile economic development and the quality of the environment, the pressures from leisure demands, and the requirement to strike the right balance between incentive and regulation, apply especially on the coast. The coastal zone, with its interaction between land and sea also presents particular problems.

Following publication in 1992 of Planning Policy Guidance note 20, *Coastal Planning* (PPG20), we set up the Coastal Forum in 1994 to bring together all the major interests in constructive dialogue, and in the autumn of 1995 we will publish policy guidelines for the coast. We have also commissioned a best practice guide for coastal zone management and initiated a review of coastal byelaws. Together, these represent a significant package of measures designed to promote sustainable development on our coasts.

Quality of Development

Proposals for new development can attract strong local opposition, leading to conflict between those who value the benefits which the development could bring and those who attach greater priority to protecting the environment. However, at their best new buildings can enhance the environment, adding to a sense of place and local identity. This message is central to the "Quality in Town and Country" initiative which we launched in 1994 and which has received widespread public support.

High Barn Cottages, Warnford, Hampshire (Architects: Radley House Partnership)

Radley House Partnership

129

Countryside Commission

Sensitively designed petrol station at Colesbourne, Gloucestershire

Historically, building styles were a reflection of local conditions and local materials. Today, improved transport and manufacturing techniques make it possible to build the same standard house in any part of the country. There is a danger that everywhere housing developments will end up looking the same and that local character will be lost.

The response to the discussion document on Quality in Town and Country and to the Rural White Paper consultation revealed strong support for the principle that new development in the countryside should contribute to a sense of local identity and regional diversity. The Government too endorses this principle. Modern designs in the countryside can and should be responsive to local character, reflect local building styles and enhance the environment. This does not mean that new buildings should slavishly imitate designs of the past, but simply that they should respect their setting and their neighbours. They need to be designed as the heritage of the future, the buildings by which our generation will be remembered, taking their place naturally among the products of the past.

These concerns are reflected in recent work by the Countryside Commission on ways of understanding and influencing the design of development in rural areas. The Commission has shown how it is possible for local people to become involved in developing guides to village design. It is also promoting the development by local planning authorities of design summaries at district level. **We will now discuss with the Commission ways of promoting the preparation of village design statements throughout England, and encouraging the preparation of countryside design summaries.**

In June 1995, as part of the "Quality in Town and Country" initiative, we launched an "Urban Design Campaign" to promote debate about how the design of streets and buildings should relate to the form, layout and character of the local area. This campaign, which should apply to villages as well as towns and cities, aims to stimulate new thinking about how development can improve local areas, not only economically but also environmentally. **The results will also contribute to good practice guidance which we intend to issue in 1996 on the processes that lead to good design.**

Award schemes too can show how sensitive development can make a positive contribution to the landscape. Jointly with the National House Building Council and the Royal Institute of British Architects (RIBA), the Department of the Environment (DOE) sponsors Housing Project Awards and Housing Design Awards for new housing in both urban and rural areas. In 1995 the Rural Development Commission also sponsored a special rural housing award in the Civic Trust Awards. **In partnership with RIBA, DOE will now complement these schemes by launching a new competition to encourage sensitive design of new low cost homes for first time buyers in rural areas.**

We intend to take a number of further steps to improve the quality of building in the countryside and will:

- revise Planning Policy Guidance note 1, *General Policy and Principles,* to encourage a more regionally and locally based approach to design and planning. This will enable local authorities to recognise and value what is distinctive in their area and guide new development accordingly;

- advise local planning authorities on the scope for making planning permission conditional on removal of ugly or derelict buildings;

- remind local planning authorities of the importance of thoroughly checking the genuineness of developments to be carried out under agricultural permitted development rights. We will take additional steps to prevent the abuse of agricultural permitted development rights, whilst ensuring that unnecessary additional burdens are not placed on genuine farmers;

- conserve the distinctive character of small communities by promoting best practice in traffic calming, building on the work of the Village Speed Control Working Group;

- ensure that any major new roads which are necessary are located with sensitivity and landscaped effectively;

- ensure that new local roads, and associated footpaths, cycleways and signs are designed and built to standards appropriate to their rural location, reconsidering, as necessary, relevant official advice and requirements which influence their design.

Housing

The demand for large scale housing development, a result more of changes in our lifestyle than of our growing population, is placing increasing pressures on our countryside. Over the last century our population has doubled but the number of houses has quadrupled, reflecting a substantial decline in average household size. People live longer and live in their own houses longer, they leave home for a place of their own earlier and, sadly, marriages break up far more often. We have not yet counted the social cost of these changes - particularly of the last, which lays extensive burdens upon society and upon the environment. Projections suggest[1] that there may be 4.4 million extra households in England by 2016, compared with 1991 - that is almost one extra household for every four in 1991. This does not necessarily mean 4.4 million extra homes, but there is clearly a need for a substantial amount of land for new housing.

We encourage development to take place wherever possible on land which has previously been developed, rather than on greenfield sites. In 1992, an estimated 47% of new residential development was on previously developed land, compared with 42% in 1989 and 38% in 1985. However, recycling of developed land cannot meet all future demand for housing.

In response to these pressures, our policies for meeting new housing needs are based on a number of principles:

- make best use of existing housing. The Housing White Paper[2], published in June 1995, sets out a number of measures to make best use of existing housing. These include incentives to encourage elderly people to move out of large houses into smaller units and to encourage more people to rent spare rooms to lodgers. The White Paper also sets a target for a reduction in the number of vacant properties managed by public authorities;

- make best use of land which has already been developed. Before building on green field sites, the full potential of derelict and degraded land should be exploited. We have set a target for the year 2005 of building half of all new homes on re-used sites. These include redundant developments in the countryside, such as defence bases which are no longer needed, as well as sites in inner cities. In recognition of the additional expense that can be incurred, the

1 *Projections of Households in England to 2016: Department of the Environment, 1995, HMSO*

2 *Our Future Homes: Opportunity, Choice, Responsibility: The Government's Housing Policies for England and Wales; Department of the Environment, 1995, HMSO*

Government provides funding to English Partnerships and through the Single Regeneration Budget Challenge Fund to help subsidise development on sites which would not otherwise be economic and would be left derelict;

- make cities more attractive places to live. Improving the quality of life for those who live and work in our cities will also help to reduce the pressure of development on the countryside. This White Paper has already described a number of measures designed to make cities more attractive places, including regeneration programmes, resources to improve existing housing, the campaign to improve the quality of urban design and our plans for new national best practice on urban greening. As a way of revitalising run down parts of cities, we are also keen to encourage mixed developments which provide a range of housing, from the affordable to the luxurious, alongside commercial and retail property. However, there are limits to the amount of housing which cities can accommodate without becoming overcrowded;

- focus new development on existing centres of population. In order to protect the open countryside and to reduce the need to travel by car, Planning Policy Guidance note 13, *Transport,* aims to focus development on urban and rural centres which offer access to a range of services and opportunities and which are readily accessible by means other than the car;

- consider how best to accommodate the rising number of households as people live longer and in smaller family units. The extent to which urban areas can accommodate new development varies from place to place. In some areas only a limited amount of new development will be possible without destroying the character and quality of the local environment. The creation of new, well designed towns and villages of differing sizes which contribute to sustainable development may be part of the solution to the need for new housing. We will produce a discussion paper which will consider the options for accommodating necessary housing development. We hope to stimulate a public debate on these issues, which concern us all, and to establish a measure of consensus on possible ways forward.

If undeveloped land needs to be developed, any adverse effects on the environment should be minimised. In accordance with the principles of sustainable development, we remain committed to protecting the best and most versatile agricultural land as a national resource for future generations. This is defined as land in grades 1, 2 and 3a of our Agricultural Land Classification. We now intend to clarify the weight to be attached to the agricultural importance of grade 3a land, making clear that a more flexible approach may be adopted in areas where, for example, there is little land in lower grades. This will enable us to take fuller account of the environmental consequences of different development options where there is a choice between developing grade 3a land and other land which may be of a lower agricultural classification but of significant landscape, wildlife or amenity value.

TRANSPORT

Rural businesses and communities need to have reasonable access to goods, services and other people, and an adequate road network is part of the solution. In many rural areas cars are more of a necessity than in cities. It is not a practical option, for example, to have a frequent bus service for all rural communities, including the most remote and sparsely populated. Our policies have to start from these realities and recognise the importance of the car to people in the countryside. However, we also need to accept that increasing levels of traffic, and the road development associated with it, bring real environmental problems.

In both urban and rural areas, increased prosperity and better roads have led to significant increases in car use. Because in the past there has been a strong apparent correlation between economic growth and traffic growth, the Government's National Road Traffic Forecasts anticipate an increase in total traffic of between 61% and 98% by 2025, compared with 1993. If these sorts of trends were to become a reality, the steepest increases in traffic, especially in leisure and commuting traffic, would probably take place in the countryside, with unacceptable consequences in many areas.

M6 motorway at Lune Valley, Cumbria which won a Civic Trust Award

John Tomkins/Environment Picture Library

Our objectives are to improve the choice and quality of transport for all those who live and work in the countryside and to reduce the adverse impact of transport on the rural environment. How these objectives can best be reconciled is not just for Government to judge. It is a question which concerns everyone. The Secretary of State for Transport has therefore launched a national debate on transport priorities with the aim of reaching a greater consensus on where the balance should lie. In practice solutions are likely to vary considerably between different parts of the country, both between city and countryside and between different rural areas, in response to the diversity of living patterns and priorities. The views of those who live in the countryside will be important in helping to determine the future shape of transport policy. **We will publish a report drawing together our conclusions from this national debate.**

In some cases the right answer will be to improve roads, where it is economically justified or where the volume of traffic has become a hazard to health or safety, but we recognise that some new roads can result in increased levels of traffic. The trunk roads programme was reviewed in 1994. The revised programme aims to relieve congestion, before the economic and environmental costs become too high, and to help improve the quality of life in rural areas by:

- targeting expenditure on motorway and trunk road improvements and much needed bypasses of towns and villages;

- reducing proposals for building new trunk routes, particularly those which go through the open countryside;

- withdrawing some schemes with particular environmental disadvantages or which are unlikely to be developed in the foreseeable future, thereby reducing blight and uncertainty.

We also encourage planning polices which will help reduce the need to travel in the longer term by bringing employment and services closer to people. Planning Policy Guidance note 13, *Transport*, advises local planning authorities to strengthen the rôle and character of villages and market towns in ways which will minimise the need for travel. Reducing the need to travel is more difficult to achieve in rural areas than in large towns. **We are publishing a best practice guide to Planning Policy Guidance note 13 which will show how local authorities can encourage developments which make more imaginative and efficient use of public transport.**

Traffic Management

Traffic calming has to date been used most widely in towns and cities but it can also make a significant improvement to the quality of life in villages by slowing traffic down as it passes through. In some circumstances this can be a cheaper and more desirable alternative to a bypass, or a valuable complementary measure. We therefore encourage wider use of traffic calming measures by the highway authority in villages where speeding traffic is a problem.

In 1994, we published the results of a study by the Village Speed Control Working Group, a collaborative initiative with the County Surveyors' Society. This investigated ways of controlling the speed of vehicles passing through 24 villages, 19 of which were in England. The study found that a mixture of gateways and complementary measures could achieve major reductions in speeds. The Department of Transport is carrying out further studies of traffic calming schemes and monitoring their success. It will continue to disseminate advice on the most effective practices to highway authorities.

It is important for traffic calming measures to be sensitive to the character of their surroundings. Too often schemes have been introduced without adequate consultation, often by those with urban experience and little knowledge or concern for rural interests. Consultation with local residents and parish councils will help to promote acceptance of the measures. This will be most useful where it gives a clear impression of their visual impact. We will therefore work with local authorities to develop effective local consultation procedures and traffic calming designs which are in keeping with the local environment. Great care must be taken to see that the signs which are used are well designed, in keeping with the character of their surroundings, and as few as possible to achieve their purpose.

On certain country roads the use of traffic calming and traffic management techniques could create a safer environment for walking, cycling or horseriding. These roads could also be the focus for methods of roadside verge management to encourage a greater variety of wild flowers and birdlife.

Highways authorities can do much to help bring about these improvements by looking at their network of rural roads to determine which roads might be suitable and developing a closer dialogue with parish councils and rural communities in designing sensitive traffic calming measures. We will invite the Countryside Commission to work in close partnership with the Department of Transport, highways authorities, parish councils and local communities to develop pilot projects which will test out the feasibility of this approach and ways of implementing it effectively.

It is estimated that some 30% of car mileage in Britain is for leisure purposes. Cars are used for nearly 80% of our holiday trips and by 20% of visitors from continental Europe. Some of this traffic puts pressure on the most attractive parts of our countryside. Our policies to enhance recreational opportunities close to where people live should have the effect of reducing visitor pressure, but traffic management in some areas is also necessary to prevent tourism from destroying the environmental resource on which it depends.

National Park authorities are among the first to explore possible solutions. Dartmoor National Park, for example, plans to expand summer public transport to include additional routes and to extend the season. The Park authority has produced a guide to local walks which link in with the enhanced public transport network.

The Lake District Traffic Management Project

Initiated in 1993 by the Lake District National Park, in partnership with the Countryside Commission, Cumbria County Council and the English Tourist Board, this project aims to protect the countryside from traffic pressure by reducing visitors' dependence on their cars. Amongst the proposals to improve public transport are:

- a brochure to explain the strategy to the public;

- a new map and public transport travel guide;

- introduction of a restricted parking zone, an access prohibition and advisory speed limits to test traffic management measures.

Following public consultation this summer on the wider context of the project, the partners are considering further proposals, including some experimental schemes. These include a review of the current road hierarchy in order to determine the routes most suitable for use by cyclists, coaches, caravans and others. Other proposals include bus and boat connections and 20 mph speed limits for country roads.

Cycling

Cycling should be an integral part of a sustainable transport policy. We therefore intend to work closely with local authorities and cycling groups to develop a national cycling strategy and to consider targets to increase the use of bicycles. The strategy will include measures to improve safety for cyclists on the roads and to provide more secure parking spaces for cycles. We will hold discussions, followed by a national conference in 1996 to promote the new strategy. It will be important to ensure that the rural dimension is fully appreciated.

Cyclists at Hawkshead, Lake District

David Townend/Environment Picture Library

The National Cycle Network

This project aims to create a network of safe and attractive cycle routes reaching into all areas of mainland Britain. Half of its mileage will be traffic free routes for shared use by cyclists, walkers and people with disabilities, while the other half will be on traffic calmed and minor roads. The network will extend through both urban and rural areas, enhancing public access to the countryside. Launched by Sustrans in 1994 as a 5,000 mile network, the enthusiasm of local authorities and other partners has boosted the total planned mileage beyond 6,000. Sustrans will receive £42.5 million towards the cost of the network from the Millenium Commission with money raised from the National Lottery.

Road Lighting

Excessive lighting on some rural roads and in village streets is a concern to many rural residents. Lighting apparatus can spoil daytime views, while the light itself can shut out the splendour of the night sky. We believe that the intrusiveness of rural lighting should be kept to the minimum necessary for safety and that highways authorities should apply this principle to new roads or bypasses in the open countryside, taking the opportunity provided by road improvements to remove unnecessary lighting. There is also considerable scope for improving design standards for lighting and varying light levels where these are inappropriate for rural settings.

Some work has already been done to mitigate the harmful effects of rural lighting. The Department of Transport's Good Roads Guide[1] includes guidance on lighting, while the Countryside Commission published a research report[2] in June 1995 on the design of rural roads, which includes guidance on lighting. **We will ask the Countryside Commission to commission further research which will lead to a best practice guide on lighting for rural roads.**

NATURAL RESOURCES

Mike Jackson/Environment Picture Library

Windfarm at disused RAF airfield at Haverigg Cumbria, operated by Windcluster Ltd of Oxford and Powergen

Energy

The countryside has traditionally provided most of the energy on which society depends. For most of this century, Britain's economy was largely coal based, and coal mining was a major rural industry. Even though recent years have seen the development of oil and gas fields off-shore, as part of a diversification of fuel production, the way in which energy is produced and supplied still has a major influence on the landscape. The scale of nuclear and coal fired power stations for example and the environmental impact of open cast coal mines or of electricity pylons are the result of our demand for energy.

Liberalisation of the electricity industry promotes efficiency of supply by introducing competition and subjecting investments to market criteria. This in turn is encouraging the development of smaller, gas fired power stations which require much less intrusive infrastructure than coal fired ones. We are also encouraging the development of local generating plants, closer to their customers, for example using Combined Heat and Power technology.

Electricity pylons however are one of the most unpopular environmental effects of power generation. It is generally prohibitively expensive to dismantle pylons and put power lines underground but measures to increase local generation can reduce the need for cross country power lines, and the justification for any new transmission lines, and the resultant environmental impact, has to be rigorously demonstrated before the necessary planning permission will be given. The Electricity Act 1989 requires the Director General of Electricity Supply to have regard to the environment, and in a number of cases, he has approved the extra cost of putting new power lines underground.

There is great scope for consumers of energy to meet their needs while using energy more efficiently. This will be both of economic benefit to them and of environmental benefit to the countryside. We have therefore increased the budget of the Energy Efficiency Office by 50% in three years and helped to establish the Energy Saving Trust to work in partnership with the industry to promote energy efficiency among consumers and small businesses.

---

[1] *The Good Roads Guide forms the first three sections in Volume 10 of the Design Manual for Roads and Bridges, Department of Transport, 1993, HMSO.*
[2] *Roads in the Countryside, Countryside Commission, 1995, ISBN 0 86 170431 2*

The generation of energy from renewable sources has a growing potential to serve the needs of smaller rural communities in ways which minimise environmental pollution. Renewable energy sources are currently supplying about 2% of the UK electricity supply, but it has been estimated that by 2025 the proportion could rise to between 5% and 20%. Many of these projects may be located in the countryside.

In particular, Britain has the opportunity of harnessing wind energy to produce electricity. Wind farms have become quite a common sight in the countryside, and further ones are planned. However, concerns have been expressed about their impact on the landscape. Wind farms have a valuable contribution to make provided they are located with sensitivity. Planning Policy Guidance note 22, *Renewable Energy*, gives advice to local planning authorities on all forms of renewable energy and includes detailed guidance on the siting of wind farms. The British Wind Energy Association also published guidelines for its members in 1994 on the sensitive siting of wind farms.

Renewable Energy

Two commercial power stations fuelled by chicken litter have recently opened at Diss in East Anglia and Glanford in South Humberside, supplying electricity to the national grid. They each directly employ about 20 staff, and also provide indirect employment for a further 15 to 20 people. They provide a welcome disposal outlet for farm waste and contribute about £1.5 million to the local economy. Further similar plants are planned.

Chicken litter power station

Minerals

A wide range of minerals are worked in England for construction, energy and other industrial purposes. Mineral extraction is an essentially rural activity, and an important source of jobs, many of which are in parts of the countryside where other stable employment is scarce. But the working of minerals can have severe environmental impacts and can be particularly intrusive in the most beautiful landscapes. Our objectives are therefore to encourage:

Restored gravel pit, Spucle Oak Lake, Marlow, Buckinghamshire, now an important site for wildfowl

● a more sustainable approach to minerals extraction;

● the reclamation of sites when extraction or waste tipping is completed.

Sustainable development means that we should reduce our reliance on primary aggregates and make more use of recycled materials and of secondary materials, such as colliery spoil, china clay waste and slate waste. Our Minerals Planning Guidance note 6, *Guidelines for Aggregates Provision in England*, sets targets for this. **We are inviting industry to develop proposals on how these targets can be met and will monitor progress.**

We are also exploring ways of increasing recycling of minerals. In particular, the construction and repair of roads consumes some 30% of all aggregates. The Departments of Environment and Transport have jointly commissioned research into ways of increasing the use of secondary and recycled materials in this work.

Many operators were given permission to extract minerals in earlier decades when environmental standards were more lax. We now expect all minerals operations to meet modern standards so that they are less intrusive in the countryside and sites are restored to beneficial uses when extraction or tipping is completed. The Environment Act 1995 requires mineral operators or owners of sites who were granted permission between 1948 and 1982 to submit new schemes for the operation, restoration and aftercare of their sites for the approval of the mineral planning authority. All sites will be subject to review and updating every 15 years.

There is great potential for the restoration of mineral sites to make a positive contribution to the countryside. Our policies encourage progressive restoration wherever possible. We look to the minerals industry to minimise the visual impact of workings on the countryside and to create landforms which blend into the local landscape or which provide new and attractive landscape features. Site reclamation should create wildlife habitats or areas of recreational interest, ensure that higher quality agricultural land is restored to its former standard or provide new woodland. Between 1988 and 1994 almost 17,000 hectares were reclaimed in these ways.

Soil

Soil is a vital resource. It is essential for plant growth, for the production of the complex molecules on which life depends, in maintaining wildlife habitats, as a reservoir for water and as a sink for carbon. It also acts as a buffer and filter for pollutants. Our objective is to ensure that land use policies and land management practices use this resource sustainably, preventing unnecessary loss and maintaining its quality. We will study carefully the report by the Royal Commission on Environmental Pollution on environmental problems associated with soil, which is expected by the end of 1995.

Water

The English rural landscape has been shaped by water and our management of it, from the glaciated valleys of the Lake District to the highly managed landscapes and ecologies of the Somerset Levels and the reclaimed fields of Romney Marsh. Most towns too are dependent on the countryside for their water resources.

A high quality water environment often has economic benefit. For example it can add to commercial and residential property values, improve opportunities for angling and, by sustaining wildlife and an attractive landscape, it can add to the tourist potential of the countryside. Water is also an essential resource for industry, power generation and irrigation as well as for drinking. The exceptional weather of the summer of 1995 with its long periods of drought and high temperatures, reminded us all of the key importance of water as a resource rather than a commodity.

Reed beds and windmill at Wicken Fen, Cambridgeshire

Sally Morgan/Ecoscene

Ministry of Agriculture, Fisheries and Food

Cuckmere, South Downs

So the water environment needs to be managed sustainably to meet a number of different objectives, including:

- conserving plants and wildlife both in the water and nearby;

- underpinning tourism and recreation, including angling, as well as commercial and residential property values;

- providing the water needed for many uses, such as domestic consumption, industry, agriculture, horticulture and fish farming.

In some areas there may not in the longer term be enough water to meet all these different uses. There can also be conflicts between different economic activities, for example between the needs of farming and fishing, and between water sports and the protection of wildlife. We need to reconcile competing priorities so that the use of water is sustainable and it serves the different purposes for which it is used.

Water Resources

England does not have universally the levels of rain which we might imagine. In the Eastern counties the average annual rainfall per head of population is less than the average in France. It is not surprising then that in some parts of England water is not always a plentiful resource and it needs to be used sustainably. Thanks to the water cycle, water is not permanently lost and in general it should be possible to arrange to meet demand for its use, provided that the full costs of supply are met. Those costs are very substantial, and there can also be significant environmental costs of reservoirs and withdrawing water from rivers. Environmental costs need to be properly taken into account in decisions.

As living standards rise and demand for domestic use continues to increase, there are likely to be local shortfalls in the Thames, Southern, Anglian and Severn Trent regions by 2021, even after developing local resources to the full. Additional resources can be opened up by building new reservoirs, by drawing on aquifers not yet fully utilised or through inter-regional transfers. New reservoirs of course can bring environmental and recreational benefits, but they take up land and can drown valuable landscapes, wildlife habitats and even villages, and these factors need to be taken into account. Pumping from aquifers can have unacceptable impacts on river flow, particularly in chalk areas and transfers can have undesirable ecological impacts as a result of introducing water having different chemical characteristics.

We believe that everyone should use water responsibly and avoid waste in order to delay the need for new water resources. In particular:

- "Water Conservation: Government Action"[1], published in August 1995, sets out the water conservation measures which we believe should be taken following consultation on our paper "Using Water Wisely".

- the National Rivers Authority and the Director General of Water Services are using their powers to require water companies to minimise leakage. The Director General expects water companies to set themselves demanding targets for reducing leakage. We have said that if voluntary targets prove ineffective we shall consider using the power to make these mandatory. Research and trials have shown that meters can cut the use of water by up to 20%, partly by eliminating leakage from customers' own pipes. The National Rivers Authority and the Director General are encouraging increased use of meters in areas of water shortage. New dwellings are metered in most areas. For existing domestic users metering will normally be on a voluntary basis, but in the interests of encouraging sustainable use, our view is that priority should be given to metering high usage outside the home;

- the Environment Act 1995 places a statutory duty on water companies to promote efficient use of the water they supply, and gives the Director General of Water Services a power to set standards of performance by water companies in promoting the efficient use of water;

- we are reviewing the arrangements for regulating water abstractions with a view to publishing proposals for changes. We also propose to publish a discussion paper on the scope for using economic instruments to encourage sustainable patterns of abstraction. Both the system of regulation and economic instruments are relevant to the question of deciding on competing demands for the use of water resources, between for example public supply, industry and agriculture.

[1] *Water Conservation: Government Action, Department of the Environment, 1995*

Water Quality

Surface water supports fishing, recreation, abstraction for irrigation and drinking water, and it is important for the conservation of aquatic flora and fauna. Successive governments have long pursued a policy of maintaining and improving surface water quality. There are now domestic and international controls over point source discharges, for example from industry and sewage treatment works; over pollution from diffuse sources, such as farmland; and over the potentially most dangerous substances. For its part, industry invests in equipment to control water pollution, while the sewerage companies are spending over £1 billion a year in ways that benefit surface water quality.

As a result of these measures, salmon and other species are returning to stretches of river where they have not been seen for over a century. Some 90% of rivers in England and Wales are of good or fair quality - a much higher proportion than the average for Europe as a whole. National Rivers Authority monitoring shows that in England and Wales between 1990 and 1994 there was a net improvement in class by river length of 26%.

We all share responsibility for the countryside and can take action which will help shape and secure its future.

Individuals

Everyone can:

- protect the countryside by using natural resources prudently, such as water, energy and minerals;

- as consumers, encourage retailers to stock produce grown in environmentally friendly ways;

- as visitors, recognise our obligation to respect the rural ways of life and the fact that for many the countryside is their home and place of work;

- help conserve the rural environment, for example by observing the Country Code and choosing to use our cars less.

Local residents can:

- support activities to help strengthen the local community;

- participate in local institutions such as the parish council;

- acknowledge that rural areas must continue to adapt to change if they are to thrive;

- use local services, for example the village shop and bus services;

- as governors, teachers and parents help keep village schools open, for example by making their premises available for community activities;

- participate in a Neighbourhood Watch scheme or serve as a neighbourhood constable.

Volunteers and voluntary groups can:

- work with local and national government to help ensure that programmes are responsive to the needs of rural people and the environment;

- help to assess local needs and priorities, for example by organising village appraisals and design statements and local housing and transport surveys;

- take part in informal activities, such as giving lifts and doing shopping for a neighbour;

- participate in voluntary schemes, for example through monitoring bird populations or repairing footpaths.

Businesses

Businesses create the wealth which enables the countryside to thrive. While maximising their efficiency and exploiting the opportunities offered by, for example, new technologies, TECs and Business Links, rural businesses can:

- ensure that their production systems and other operations and those of their suppliers are as environmentally sensitive as possible;

- ensure that any new development is of an appropriate design and scale for its location;

- consider how best to undertake their activities in ways that are sensitive to the needs and wishes of local people.

Different businesses can play their part:

- housing developers can provide a range of housing to help maintain mixed communities and ensure that new designs reflect the locality;

- retailers can market produce which has been grown using environmentally friendly farming methods;

- rural shopkeepers can offer a range of goods and services to local people where they would otherwise be unavailable.

Farmers and Land Managers

Farmers, foresters and land managers look after 80% of the land. Their contribution is vital, because Government regulation and control is not enough in itself to conserve the beauty and diversity of our environment. They can:

- combine their essential food producing rôle with the protection of wildlife habitats and the landscape;

- act as stewards of our countryside while running efficient, competitive and modern businesses.

Parish Councils

Parish Councils can play an important rôle in the local community. In particular, they can:

- make best use of their existing powers, for example by playing a more active rôle in the management of footpaths within their areas;

- play a stronger rôle in crime prevention and community transport, subject to consultation and legislation;

- take an increasing rôle in pressing the views of the local community, for example to National Park authorities.

District and County Councils

District and county councils have an important rôle in shaping rural development and the delivery of services. They need to be sensitive to the local characteristics of their area and the particular needs of rural residents. District and county councils and other public sector service providers can look to adopt, where appropriate, the guidance which will be issued as part of the Rural Charter initiative.

District and county councils can:

- prepare and update Rural Strategies which build on consultation with local people to set out an integrated approach to policies for rural areas;

- promote community development and support community involvement in local decision making, for example by delegating appropriate responsibilities to parish councils;

- use the resources made available from the sale of county farms to support rural initiatives;

- cooperate with local bodies to compile registers of rural buildings with unimplemented planning permission for economic uses;

- prepare Community Safety Strategies which help prevent rural crime.

Through the planning system district and county councils can:

- reflect the value people place on the distinctive character of their area, without applying designations which unduly discourage development;

- encourage development which respects the environment and responds to local character;

- inform unsuccessful applicants for planning permission what forms of development are acceptable under the development plan;

- reduce the need to travel by focusing new development on existing centres which are readily accessible by means other than the car and by encouraging more recreational activities close to where people live;

- encourage wherever possible new building on land which has already been developed;

- help maintain the vitality of market towns and villages, for example by considering the impact on local shops of major new retail developments.

District and county councils can provide and manage transport in rural areas. Specifically they can:

- develop innovative ways of providing public transport, for example by making more flexible use of school buses;

- work with the Post Office and parish councils to provide new post buses;

- encourage people to make more journeys by bicycle;

- promote the wider use of traffic calming measures in consultation with local residents;

- control or prohibit the use of vehicles on some rights of way.

Those district and county councils with responsibility for housing can:

- produce and regularly update rural housing policies to encourage communities of mixed age and income;

- ensure that best use is made of existing stock, by seeking to reduce underoccupation;

- encourage conversions in order to meet the growing need for housing small households.

National Government

This White Paper sets the framework for sustainable development in the countryside. It includes measures to:

- enable rural businesses to develop and contribute to the national economy;

- help to ensure that people in the countryside have access to high quality public services;

- conserve the character of the countryside - its landscape, wildlife, agricultural, recreational and natural resource value;

- encourage active communities which take the initiative to solve their problems.

We have set ourselves the task of responding to the particular needs of rural areas and considering the rural dimension of particular policies. To achieve this we will:

- consider rural dimensions of policies across government by expanding the remit of the Cabinet Committee dealing with the environment so that it will consider rural affairs;

- charge this Committee with ensuring speedy progress in implementing the commitments in this White Paper;

- report on progress next year;

- ensure that Government Offices for the Regions remain sensitive to rural concerns by meeting regularly with representatives of rural communities and by working closely with our countryside agencies, the Forestry Commission and the MAFF regional organisation.

This White Paper contains proposals in a number of areas which will carry forward the public debate on the future of our countryside. In formulating new policies, we will take full account of the views of rural people. We shall consult on:

- proposals to introduce a Rural Business Use Class to encourage new business development which is appropriate to the countryside;

- the introduction of a new scheme to provide rate relief to village shops;

- the introduction of new powers for parish councils to strengthen their role in community transport and crime prevention;

- the operation of environmental land management schemes, through a new national forum and arrangements in each region;

- measures to improve the management of common land;

- ways of making changes to the Rights of Way network simpler and more flexible, following a pilot project to increase the involvement of parish councils in the management of footpaths;

- draft regulations to protect important hedgerows;

- draft revision of Planning Policy Guidance note 7 *The Countryside and the Rural Economy;*

- options for ways of accommodating the rising number of households.

Printed in the United Kingdom for HMSO
Dd. 5067008. 10/95 C50. 48003 51-8542. ORD 335573.